To
Mitzi, Martha, Kathleen, Roger, Frank, Kim, Emily, Tim,
and
to Constance Forsyth,
whose love for our language has always been an inspiration.

# Contents

## Part III
## BECOMING A GLOBAL COMMUNICATOR

# Acknowledgments

In the Appendix of this book you will find ways to say "thank you" in six different languages. I would like to use *all* of them to thank the following people:

My wife, Mitzi; her mother, Mrs. F; and my good friend Dick Rosenberg—all of whom took the time to carefully read and comment on the manuscript for this book.

Maria Meyer-Netto, graduate student in journalism at the University of Wisconsin (Madison), for her extensive and useful research and reporting.

Mike Fornwald, illustrator, who has now brightened four of my books.

P J Dempsey, Senior Editor at John Wiley & Sons, who entrusted me with this assignment.

Sally Wecksler, my literary agent, who assisted me in rolling what I hope will be this lucky seventh.

Three prominent Britishers who vetted Chapter 4, on the differences between American English and English English: Ian Kerr, who heads his own public relations firm in Greenwich, Connecticut; Reg Abbiss, who is a public relations executive with Rolls Royce Motor Cars; and Norma Davis, who is a journalist in Wesport, Connecticut.

Two people I have never met but greatly admire: Richard Lederer, author of several wonderful books on the English language; and Edward T. Hall, noted social anthropologist and expert on other cultures.

Ad Hoc Translations, Inc., a national translation service with offices in New York and Los Angeles (phone 212/979-2816). My thanks to Maria Zadunaisky and Bernard Liller for their support and assistance.

William Lutz, who teaches English at Rutgers University, is author of the delightful book *Doublespeak*, and is chairperson of the National Committee on Public Doublespeak.

Two institutions that provided volumes of information on cross-cultural communication: The David M. Kennedy International Center at Brigham Young University, and V. Lynn Tyler; and The Intercultural Press Inc., Yarmouth, Maine. If the subject of cross-cultural communication interests you, I urge you to write both of these first-class institutions and obtain catalogs listing their many publications.

I also wish to thank some wonderful people in scores of audiences across the United States and overseas during the past ten years. Following my after-dinner, keynoter, or seminar programs, they freely shared anecdotes and personal experiences about language that evoked a smile and illustrated a point, and then brightened a page in this book.

Roger E. Axtell

# Introduction

A recent survey conducted by *USA Today,* the national newspaper, posed this question: "What is your biggest worry as an international traveler?"

The following nine "worry" categories were listed:

| | |
|---|---|
| personal safety | getting lost |
| lost baggage | hotel room theft |
| well-being of family | plane bombing/hijacking |
| inability to communicate | connections or delays |
| illness | |

The result was that the *number one* fear—ranking almost three times greater than the second-place fear—was inability to communicate. In second place came personal safety.

If you share that concern, if you are troubled or worried about communicating with people in other parts of the world, then this book will help you. You will learn—while laughing—about the strengths and weaknesses of American English. You will also learn how to become more sensitive and aware when speaking or listening to English, and how to avoid misstatements, language goofs, gaffes, *faux pas* (French for "mistakes") and *faux amis* (or "false friends," meaning words in another language that look the same as English words but mean entirely different things) when attempting to communicate around the world.

## THE LANGUAGE PROBLEM

Anthropologists tell us that language—both spoken and written—is what lifts humans above the animal kingdom. "We take language for granted," writes Dr. Richard M. Restak, author of *The Mind* (Bantam, 1988), "yet it is one of the most complex things we do. Language allows us to convey our emotions, to share ideas, to create fresh forms of expression, and to communicate our most intimate thoughts." Restak also posits that "the need to communicate with other humans through language seems as fundamental as the existence of the mind itself."

Now comes the kicker: There are about five thousand *different* languages in the world today, and English is just one of them.

Meanwhile, not only are most Americans monolingual, but our brand of English—American English—has evolved into a special *dialect* that reflects the American obsession with idioms, slang, jargon, buzz words, acronyms, and sports and military terminology. Today, two Americans can carry on a conversation that others in the so-called English-speaking world might barely comprehend. And if our English-speaking cousins can't understand us, pity all those people out there struggling to learn English.

Furthermore, American English is growing more complex at an exponential pace. Pick up a newspaper and you'll find (as I did in yesterday's paper) words like *Scram!* or *cockamamie* or *dis* or *wonk* or expressions like *What's your take on that, Mr. President?* As a reader, you don't raise an eyebrow. Now imagine an international visitor trying to make sense of those words . . . or trying to decipher our fast-paced, slurred speech: A gas station attendant inquiring "Fillerup?" . . . or a server in a restaurant asking "Watchawanonnit?" (Translation: "What do you want on your sandwich?"), and then delivering the meal with "Hereyago." ("Here you go.") Go? Go where?

There's the problem. In a shrinking world where new lines of communication are multiplying each day, we Americans find ourselves inserting a lingo that clutters all those communication channels with static and incomprehension.

## HOW THIS BOOK WILL HELP YOU

This book should thoroughly sensitize you to the problems our shipmates on this "spaceship earth" encounter when trying to comprehend American English. It should also help you become a better global communicator, whether you're trying to understand English English (the language spoken in England) while on vacation or whether you're negotiating a business deal in English in Japan.

Throughout this book, the medium for attaining this new awareness about English lingo will be stories—true-life examples that illustrate how confounding our language can be. Stories are our vehicle of choice because such diverse sources as the Bible, *Sesame Street*, and Paul Harvey each have demonstrated, in their own way, that stories are an effective means to make a point. The stories in this book will offer tips, provide lessons, and present paradigms—many of which are punctuated with a smile.

Not all the stories are lighthearted, however. Some are tragically serious—like the true account of the Japanese boy visiting Baton Rouge, Louisiana, who did not comprehend the command "Freeze!" and was fatally shot.

To establish the premise that American English is difficult to export, Chapter 1 contains a series of lighthearted anecdotes, each describing some blurred facet of our multisided language. Then, Chapter 2 provides background and evidence on why American English is so difficult.

Chapter 3 returns to the entertaining aspect of American lingo by serving up a variety of memorable "mangled misstatements." This chapter shows why trying to understand American English can be like exploring a dimly lit hall of mirrors.

Chapters 4 and 5 examine the boundaries of the English-speaking world. We learn how easily an American, a Britisher, an Australian, a New Zealander, or a South African might come to blows with other English speakers because of misunderstandings in the use of our so-called common language.

Chapter 6 turns to the serious business of how to effectively use translators and interpreters. Once again, there are plenty of humorous examples to show that even the professionals suffer from foot-in-mouth disease.

Chapter 7 enters the language labyrinth of social conversation. This chapter provides pointers on how to meet, greet, and converse with people in various places around the world. It might help you the next time you find yourself tongue-tied in, say, Thailand.

"The Tower of Business Babel" is the title of Chapter 8, which contains information helpful to anyone traveling outside the United States on business. You'll find advice for dealing with everything from brand names to boardrooms to bathrooms around the world.

Chapter 9 acquaints you with confusing cognates, those *faux amis* we mentioned earlier, plus a short but practical tutorial on how people answer the phone around the world.

In Chapter 10, you'll find the payoff, the solutions, the winning formulae—a list of ten tips for communicating more effectively when dealing with anyone for whom English is a second, or third, language.

There is also a helpful appendix on what to know about other languages. Essays on six key languages are presented from light-hearted perspectives. In addition, a survival list of key words and phrases—complete with phonetic pronunciations—is provided for each of those languages.

## SUMMARY

With this book in hand, or in mind, you can eliminate "inability to communicate" as your number one fear when traveling abroad. With a little time, a bit of study, and hopefully more than a few laughs, you will be able to relegate this fear to the bottom of your list. As you travel, you can get back to worrying about more important things . . . such as if you turned the iron off before leaving home, the odds of riots or nuclear bomb threats at your destination, and whether your airline seatmate will have *both* body odor and bad breath.

Roger E. Axtell

P.S. If you would like to contribute your experiences and anecdotes when dealing internationally with our wacky language, please send them to the editor of this book: P J Dempsey, Senior Editor, Professional & Trade Division, John Wiley & Sons, Inc., 605 Third Ave., New York, NY 10158-0012.

# Part I

# UNDERSTANDING AMERICAN ENGLISH

# 1

# Exporting
# American English

We are the first truly global generation. We are able to fly farther, faster, and cheaper than any previous generation. We can pick up the phone and talk via satellite, wire, or fiber optics to any spot on the globe that has access to another phone. Among large corporations, videoconferencing is already a workaday reality. It allows us not only to converse but also to see the people we're conversing with, whether they are in Kuwait, Singapore, Osaka, or wherever. And when we communicate through these modern media, or when we travel abroad, English is the *lingua franca* for both business and tourism. We can explore almost every corner of the world and manage to communicate in English with at least someone.

The rub is that we have also messed up our language. We've managed to clutter it with a baffling mixture of idioms, slang, jargon, puns, metaphors, buzz words, allusions, euphemisms, acronyms, and sports and military terminology.

Consequently, while hundreds of millions of people around the world may be learning textbook English, we Americans have evolved a unique, ever-changing dialect, a lingo that is confounding to nonnative readers and listeners. The result is confusion, sometimes even anger; but often it's laughter, because some of the misunderstandings can be wonderfully amusing.

To document our premise—that American English is, indeed, difficult to export—we present a series of true, lighthearted stories. These will vividly introduce the common areas of communication confusion that we will tackle throughout the book.

## INTERNATIONAL TRAVEL

An American woman visiting Athens decided to order breakfast at an outdoor restaurant. She asked for scrambled eggs, and the waiter repeated, "Yes, yes. Of course. Scrambly ags." A short time later, he returned with two fried eggs, sunny side up. "No, no," she said, "I ordered them scrambled." The waiter nodded and took the eggs back to the kitchen. However, once again he returned with two fried eggs. This time the woman said slowly, but with emphasis, "No, no, scrambled . . . like this . . ." and made a distinct, quick stirring motion with her hands. Minutes later, the waiter returned bearing two fried eggs; but just before presenting them, he made two perfect pirouettes with his body, then set the plate in front of her with a satisfied grin.

**" "**

Lakshman Ratnapala, originally from Sri Lanka where English English predominates, explains that in his country the word *dickey* is used for the trunk of an automobile. With that explanation, Ratnapala tells this story: "On one of my first visits to New York City, I took a taxicab from the airport to my hotel. On arriving, I spotted the person who was waiting to meet me. Wishing to quickly retrieve my luggage, I shouted to the taxi driver, 'Quick! Open your dickey! Open your dickey!' I could not understand why the man stood there, motionless, with a weird look on his face."

**" "**

Americans visiting Germany for the first time are usually startled and amused when they see road signs proclaiming *ausfahrt* and *einfahrt*, which merely mean "exit" and "entrance." Instead of linking the words with flatulence, my elderly aunt, visiting Germany for the first time, took a different perspective. Seeing all the signs for *ausfahrt*, she remarked, "That Ausfahrt must be a very large city."

**" "**

Nan Hartman, traveling in Peru last year, asked the manager of a restaurant where she could go to wash her hands. The manager ushered her into a bathroom where some painters happened to be working. When the painters started to leave, the manager stopped them, saying, "That's O.K. Stay. She only wants to wash her hands."

**" "**

Proof that our lingo begins the moment someone visits our airports can be found in one of comedian George Carlin's routines. Carlin says that when a person approaches an American airport the first signs of greeting proclaim *Arrivals* and *Departures*. You may ask, Which am I? Am I arriving to depart? Or, am I arriving to meet someone who is departing from an airplane? Then, whether passenger or greeter, you are directed to a *gate*. What gate? It's a doorway, not a gate. Next, an attendant directs you to get *on* the airplane. As Carlin says, "I don't know about you, but I'd rather get *in* an airplane than on it." Finally, at the end of your journey, as the plane is taxiing to the gate, the flight attendant cheerfully announces, "Thank you for flying with us today, and we hope you have a safe journey to your final destination." To this Carlin replies, "As for me, I'm not ready to go to my 'final destination' just yet."

## SOCIAL CONVERSATIONS

A Korean student, armed with years of study in basic English acquired back in Seoul, was spending his first day in America as a freshman at the University of Illinois. Another student, an American, approached with a friendly smile and said, "Hi. What's the good word?" Startled, the Korean froze in his tracks. "My God!" he thought, "I don't *know* the good word. I've studied English for years, but no one told me about the good word." He shuffled away, stunned by this first encounter. Finally, he decided to solve the mystery by reversing the situation. He approached another American and tentatively repeated the question, "Hello. What's the good word?" Seconds later, after hearing the response, he was even more confused. The reason? The American had answered, "Oh, not much."

A postscript to this story is that the next day, as this same Korean student walked the campus, another American greeted him with "Hi! What's up?"

**"     "**

A midwestern woman was once employed by a Houston oil company to teach English to visitors from Mexico and the Middle East who came to Texas to learn more about the oil business. After one class was completed, a Middle Eastern gentleman asked the woman if she would join him for dinner some evening ". . . to celebrate the end of our course, and to practice my English." She agreed. On the appointed evening, her host drove up in a huge limousine and took her to the finest restaurant in Houston. His English was still incomplete, so he ordered the meal in perfect French. Further, he ordered a bottle of fine French wine, poured some into a glass, held it up to the candlelight, looked into the woman's eyes, and said, "Well . . .

up yours!" (She realized later that what he had intended to say was the common American toast "Bottoms up!")

**" "**

Kirsten Olsen is the wife of a Danish businessman, and the pair travel frequently to the United States. She speaks and writes four languages (Danish, English, German, and French). She says: "The one thing that troubles me most about American English is when people greet me by saying 'Hello, how are you?' We don't say that in Danish. We have no equivalent. So, we don't know how to respond." As cross-cultural trainer Dr. Joan Rea adds: "The irony is that when Americans ask 'How are you?' we really *don't* want to know! For example, in America if you say 'How are you?' to the check-out person at the supermarket and they stop everything and respond, 'Well, my dog is sick, and my mother-in-law's gall bladder is bothering her, and . . .' you'd think they were crazy."

**" "**

Sigal, an Israeli girl, was in the United States learning English when she turned to her friend, Andrea, and said, "One thing I don't understand about you Americans is that when you get really, really mad, you say such a *beautiful* phrase." Andrea pondered that for a moment and then said, "I don't understand. What do you mean?" "Well," Sigal explained, "when many Americans get very, very mad, I have heard them say 'Sun on a beach!'"

**" "**

Hernando Cardenas, of Bogota, Colombia once turned to me during a dinner attended by a group of Americans at local restaurant and, in Spanish, said, "This is such a memorable and enjoyable evening, I would like to propose a toast to our group. Would that be permitted?" When I quickly assured him it would be very appropriate, he added, "This is an old Colombian toast that I will try to translate into English." I urged him to proceed. To get the group's attention, he stood and raised his glass. At this particular moment, there happened to be a hush through- out the restaurant, so all the other patrons heard exactly what followed. "I should like to make a toast," Hernando declared with great ceremony. "To all of you! Today has been a marvelous day. May I say that this is the most fun I have ever had—dressed!" After a moment's silence, the entire restaurant broke out in laughter and applause. Turn- ing to me with a surprised look, Hernando asked, "Did I say that OK?" "Yes, of course," I replied. "In fact, I don't know how you possibly could have been more descrip- tive."

## CONFUSING COGNATES

For some Latins, the word *chili* does not necessarily refer to the spicy beans-and-meat dish we Americans enjoy mixing in large pots. Among many Spanish-speaking peo- ple, that word is used to describe a certain part of a man's anatomy, probably because of a resemblance to a chile pepper. Larry Greb, a marketing executive with the Johnson Wax Company in Racine, Wisconsin, tells of one occasion where he hosted one of his Latin customers at his local country club for a game of golf. As it happened, it was a cold, rainy day. After the golf game, Greb and his guest took a hot shower. As the Latin emerged from the shower, towel around his neck, another club member happened by and casually commented, "Pretty chilly." The Latin paused for a few seconds and then politely responded, "Thank you!"

*Order a dry martini in Germany and you may be served
three of them.*

**" "**

In Germany, order a dry martini and you are liable to be
served three martinis. Reason: The word *dry* sounds exactly the same as the German word *drie*, which means
"three." The word for "one" is *ein*.

**" "**

Another alarming word for Germans is the English word
*gift*. The proper German word for "gift" is *geschenk*. Not
knowing this, an American once sent a package to a
German friend and on the outside wrote "gift" several
times, hoping to avoid customs duties. Unfortunately, in
German the word *gift* means "poison."

## PRONUNCIATION

One sound in English that causes consternation among learners is
the two different ways we pronounce the letter *g*—either the "hard"

or the "soft" way. For example, the hard g appears in the word *go*, and the soft g is heard in the word *German*. If we write them phonetically, the hard g should sound like *gah* and the soft g like *jh*. With that preface, this story came from *USA Today* reporter Chris Swingle (try reading it aloud; it's more understandable that way):

An Eastern European gentleman, new to the United States, entered a McDonalds restaurant and said "I'd like a ham-bur-*jer*, please." The attendant corrected him, saying, "We pronounce that as 'ham-bur-*ger*,' with a hard g sound." "Oh, I'm sorry," the man apologized. "You see, I'm a strain-*grr* (hard g) here."

**"      "**

Hernando Cardenas, referred to earlier, claims that "English is so terribly difficult because of its delicacy in pronunciation." When asked to explain, Cardenas offered this quiz: "What do you Americans call the animal that gives us wool? (Answer: sheep) What do you call the white material you sleep between? (Answer: sheets) What do you call the small pieces of wood that fall to the ground when you carve something? (Answer: chips) What do you call something that does not cost much? (Answer: cheap) What is another word for boats? (Answer: ships)" After several more examples like this, Cardenas concluded: "You see? All of those words are so similar in sound. And we know that you have one other similar sounding word that is terribly rude . . . which we want to avoid . . . so we tend to avoid anything that even comes close!"

Now that you have in mind that infamous four-letter English word for "fecal matter," you will have some sympathy for these two true stories:

A Venezuelan businessman explained that he was in the United States for only a few months, struggling to learn English, when he was invited to an American home for dinner. Near the end of the dinner, he decided it would be gracious to propose a toast of thanks to his hosts. He stood, apologized for his poor English, and haltingly said the following: "Thank you . . . for this . . . fine . . . dinner. Thank you . . . for the . . . good . . . wine. But . . . most . . . of all . . . thank you . . . for . . . your . . . friends__t."

**" "**

My instructor in a Berlitz course was a woman from Argentina who married an American and settled in Milwaukee. She said during her early years in the United States, she was bedeviled by the nuances of English pronunciation. She confessed her worst mistake was when she attended a PTA meeting. When attendees were polled on what they would bring to a potluck dinner at school, she stood and eagerly offered to bring a chocolate sheet cake . . but unfortunately, she pronounced it as "s___t cake."

## MISUNDERSTOOD AMERICAN SLANG

San Diego travel agent Tom Cermola relates he once commented to an overseas visitor: "Did you happen to see Monday night's football game? The Chicago Bears *licked the pants off* the Detroit Lions." Later, Cermola considered, "It wasn't until I heard myself speak those words that it occurred to me, 'I wonder what image is going through my international visitor's head?'"

**"  "**

On a tragic note, in 1992, a Japanese exchange student mistakenly approached the wrong house in Baton Rouge, Louisiana, one evening looking for a party. When the owner emerged with a shotgun and ordered the student to "Freeze!" the Japanese youth misunderstood and kept moving. He was shot and killed. This led a Japanese magazine (*Mainichi*) to feature an article headlined "Learn These English Words—Or Die!" The magazine then recommended the reader learn the meaning of the following language heard on the streets of America:

- "Freeze!" (Meaning: "Don't move or you're dead.")

- "Duck!" (Meaning: "Something is flying toward you!")

- "Spread them!" (Meaning: "Raise your hands and spread your legs.")

- "Do you bang?" (Meaning: "Are you a gang member?")

- "Are you in?" (Meaning: "Are you a member of organized crime?")

**"  "**

I once sent a FAX to the manager of our company in Lima, Peru, explaining that I needed a "head count" of the personnel there. I said that I needed "a head count telling the number of people in your factory, the number of people in your office, broken down by sex," and that I needed the information immediately. He replied: "Here is your head count. Here we have thirty-five people in our factory, fifteen people in our office, five people in the hospital, *none* broken down by sex." He added a postscript that explained: "And if you really must know, our problem down here is with alcohol."

*You'll have to pardon my voice . . . I've got a frog in my throat.*

**" "**

S. J. Hayakawa, professor of semantics and former U.S. senator, enjoyed telling this story to illustrate how confusing English can be. It seems one of his international students asked about the meaning of the word *frog*. Hayakawa explained, "It's a small green amphibious animal that lives in a pond." Puzzled, the student asked, "Then why did my roommate tell me she had a frog in her throat?"

**"    "**

For decades, Danish-born pianist and humorist Victor Borge has poked fun at American English. For example, he asks, "Why is it that you say you sit *down* in the daytime, but you sit *up* at night?" Borge also tells of going to a U.S. Amtrack railway station to buy a train ticket. "One round-trip ticket, please," he said. The ticket agent asked, "To where, sir?" To which Borge replied, "Why back to here, of course."

**"    "**

Richard Lederer, in his wonderful book *Crazy English* (Pocket Books, 1991), clearly demonstrates how American English can be confusing to others. He says: "We park on driveways and drive on parkways. Our hamburger is not made out of ham. There is no grape in grapefruit, and no pine or apple in pineapple. In what other language do you think your feet can smell and your nose can run?"

With these stories as prologue, the stage is set. The drama is taking place each day, even as you read this, in hundreds of thousands of locales around the world, as travelers wander the world trying to communicate.

# 2

# Why American English Is So Difficult

*Jess Salacuse is dean of the Law School at Tufts University. During one phase of his career, he spent time in Sudan. After returning to the United States he received a letter from a Sudanese professor who obviously intended to write "Do you still have a soft spot in your heart for Sudan?" Instead, the letter read "Do you still have a soft point in your head . . . ?"*

American English, one of the world's most opulent languages with over 750,000 words, has evolved by borrowing roots from other languages and, in the process, has adopted mind-shattering, inconsistent rules for usage, pronunciation, and spelling. To further complicate the confusion, we have also developed differences in words and phrases among geographic regions within the United States. Combine all this into one language stew—which we Americans inappropriately call "English"—and others in the world find our American lingo almost indigestible.

How has this happened? What are the consequences? We'll search for answers to these loaded questions in this chapter; "loaded" because words can become like hand grenades—handled carelessly, they'll blow up in your face.

## 1066 AND ALL THAT

Let's assume we're cartographers. Our assignment is to draw a flowchart of a river showing how English grew from its first trickle to where it is today. The wellspring for the first English words bubbled up during the Dark Ages, spoken by Germanic tribes who in the fifth century invaded the island we now call Great Britain. Those first words would sound crude and unintelligible to us today.

Our map would show a lapse of five hundred years before a major new stream joined the original river. This occurred in the watershed year 1066, when Normans from the European continent crossed what is now the English Channel and conquered the Saxons. Here our map would indicate that this Norman Conquest ended the "Old English" period and launched the "Middle English" period. We would also note that this was where the first muddy water entered our historical stream of language. It caused confusion, a frequent characteristic of today's American English. Here's one example of how this happened:

> The resident Saxons had already labeled their animals as oxen, sheep, calves, deer, and so on. But, with the arrival of the Normans, the words for the *meat* of those animals was borrowed from the more gastronomically conscious French. Thus, today, we don't eat *sheep*, we eat *mutton* (from the French word for "sheep"); similarly, we eat *beef* from *oxen*, and *veal* from *calves*, and *venison* from *deer*.

After the Norman Conquest, our map would show the river of the English language twisting and meandering through the centuries until the next major change, which occurred between the years 1476 and 1776. This was when written English became more prevalent. A written language required more consistency in spelling and punctuation. As for vocabulary, words from French, Latin, and Italian came pouring into the main channel during these years. Smaller waves of new words came from the Netherlands and from as far afield as Japan, China, and what we now call Southeast Asia.

Our map would then show where the river started to divide into distinct new channels, which we could label as the "major English-speaking peoples." The two largest would be tagged "English English" and "American English," with smaller streams labeled "Australian English," "South African English," "Irish English," and so on.

The year 1776 brought the breakaway of the American colonies, and not surprisingly, American English began to veer off in its own direction. As one of our greatest American lexicographers observed, "When you come to a fork in the road . . . take it" (Yogi Berra). The result was described by George Bernard Shaw in his now famous observation: "England and America — two great nations separated by a common language." (More on the differences between English English and American English can be found in Chapter 4.)

After the hallmark year 1776, American English began to distinguish itself, as loanwords from other languages were replaced by verbal mutations from within the new culture. American English continued to evolve independently as Americans developed a special love for adding prefixes and suffixes, for turning nouns into verbs, for adopting slang and idioms, and especially for using trendy words contributed by politicians, the younger generation, and the new word professionals in advertising and journalism.

So, those first crude Germanic words uttered back in the fifth century gave birth to a progeny that now dominates the world's linguistic spectrum.

## ENGLISH SPOKEN HERE . . . AND EVERYWHERE

Here are some statistics supporting the claim that English is preeminent among languages:[1]

- A typical unabridged English dictionary lists about 500,000 words, and there are another 500,000 technical and scientific

[1]Sources: *The Story of English*, by Robert McCrum, William Cran, and Robert MacNeil, Viking, 1986; and *U.S. News & World Report.*

terms. By comparison, German has 185,000 words, and French less than 100,000.

- According to Erik V. Gunnemark's *Geolinquistic Handbook* (published by Lanstryckeriet, Gothenburg, Sweden, 1991), English is the official language for some 1.73 billion people, and there are at least another 400 million who consider English as a second or third language. (This is somewhat misleading since the *official* language of India, with its 870 million people, is English; but in fact, only about 10 percent speak English.)

- As for daily usage, consider this eclectic list:

  — Three-quarters of the world's mail, telexes, and cables use English.

  — Half of the world's technical and scientific periodicals are written in English.

  — Eighty percent of the information stored in the world's computers is in English.

  — English is the language of sports, fashion, engineering, science, and the Olympics. And, as *U.S. News & World Report* comments: "When pop singers from Hong Kong to Heidelberg ring out their songs" and "when an Argentine pilot lands his airliner in Turkey," the language being used is English.

Furthermore, an astonishing number of people around the world aspire to learn English. In Russia, there are more teachers of English than there are people in the United States who can speak Russian. And in China, there are more people learning English than there are people in the United States.

Few other languages can touch this length and breadth of daily usage. Today, adding strength to this linguistic grasp on the globe is the U.S. based Cable News Network (CNN) that, at this writing, is seen and heard each day in over 140 countries and territories. In hotels, restaurants, and homes all over the world, everything from weather forecasts to wars to women's fashions are broadcast in English to millions and millions of people whose native tongue is some other language.

The newest contributor to this epidemic comes from the MTV network. For example, its programming is seen from as far away as India, where a whole new generation of young people are learning about and imitating the music, fashion, and *words* they see and hear on this kaleidoscope of exported American culture.

That so many speak English, whether born to it or not, is perhaps represented in this single anecdote. Linguistic professor Andrew Sihler quotes a French colleague who was to present a paper at an international conference: "What is zee true international language? I know zee answer. I speak it. Eet is broken English."

## WHAT SHOULD WE CALL AMERICAN ENGLISH?

It is customary to refer to English as one language. However, there are actually two major forms of English: the mother tongue as spoken in the United Kingdom and most of its Commonwealth, and the prodigal offspring, American English.

But, interestingly, no term has yet been officially adopted to apply to the special dialect of English developed by Americans over the past two hundred years. Go to Berlitz, say you want to learn English, and they will ask, "Do you want to learn English English or American English?"

One term for the American version of English might be *Englican.* Unfortunately, that looks and sounds like the word *Anglican* which clearly refers to the official religion of the English. A better term, perhaps, would be *Amlish,* taken from the first syllable of *American* and the last syllable of *English.* Yet that comes perilously close to the word *Amish,* a religious sect primarily located in Pennsylvania.

Perhaps the best direct solution is to simply say, "I speak American."

## PLAYING THE WORD GAME

When we attempt to coin words like *Englican* and *Amlish*, we are dabbling in a favorite American pastime (almost as popular as baseball)—creating new words. The student aiming to learn American English will soon discover that our language is truly a moving target. Americans are probably more avid creators and collectors of new words than any other culture. As a result, Americans have developed a subindustry within the field of lexicography: the production of reference books dealing solely with words—new words, obscure words, technical words, groups of words (like idioms, euphemisms, allusions, etc.), and trendy words.

Here is just a sampling of such reference books.

- Paul Dickson's book *Dickson's Word Treasury* (Wiley, 1992) is described as "a connoisseur's collection of old and new, weird and wonderful, useful and outlandish words." Examples: Did you know that the indentation in the middle of your upper lip just below your nostrils is called the philtrum? Did you know that the word *drunk* holds the record for having the greatest number of synonyms—2,231?

- Richard A. Spears, an associate professor of linguistics at Northwestern University, has produced a 462-page lexicon of improper English, entitled *Slang and Euphemism, A Dictionary of Oaths, Curses, Insults, Racial Slurs, Sexual Slang and Metaphor, Drug Talk, Homosexual Lingo and Related Matters* (Signet, 1982). This reference book contains 13,500 entries and 30,000 definitions.

- John Ciardi has authored *A Browser's Dictionary, A Compendium of Curious Expressions and Intriguing Facts* (Harper & Row, 1980). Example: The word *gringo*, while generally considered a pejorative term used by Mexicans to label all North Americans, actually is based on the Greek word *griego*, which meant "to speak outlandishly, as a foreigner"; this was the derivation of the Spanish verb *gringar*; thus a person who spoke strangely was a *gringo*.

- Hugh Rawson has produced *A Dictionary of Euphemisms & Other Doubletalk* (Crown, 1981), described as "a compilation of linguistic fig leaves and verbal flourishes for artful users of the English language." Example: As a verb, the word *off* has been used ever since World War I to mean "to kill" someone; but in recent years, this has been replaced by the term *to take out* a victim.

- David Olive has zeroed in on the business world with his "Cynic's Dictionary of Corporate Jargon" entitled *Business Babble* (Wiley, 1991). (See Chapter 8, "The Tower of Business Babel" for more commentary on the wonderful words of business.)

- Before his death in 1992, Stephen Glazier labored for over seven years to produce *Word Menu* (Random House, 1992). This is a compendium of serious and sometimes offbeat grammatical fare—slang, techno-jargon, or time-honored phrases, insults, or anatomical terms—numbering 977 pages in all.

- Sid Lerner and Gary S. Belkin compiled a book entitled *Trash Cash, Fizzbos and Flatliners* (Houghton Mifflin, 1992). This is a compilation of some of the newest words and phrases generated during the late twentieth century. Examples: *Trash cash* are "advertising leaflets that are designed to look like U.S. currency"; *fizzbos* is a twisted acronym for "for sale by owner"; and *flatliners* are people "whose EKG response is recorded as a flat line; essentially, a person who is dead."

- Sylvia Cole and Abraham H. Lass have collected and explained some 900 allusions in their book *The Dictionary of 20th Century Allusions* (Fawcett, 1991). Examples: "A *gung-ho* salesman suddenly found himself in a *catch-22* situation." The meaning of that sentence is totally lost unless you know what *gung-ho* and *catch-22* signify. Similarly, saying that Ronald Reagan was a "John Wayne–type of president" is an allusion to a whole bundle of personal characteristics . . . but only if you know who John Wayne was.

- John Davis's book *Buzzwords: The Jargon of the 1990's*, (Crown, 1993) lists examples of how professional jargon has become almost unintelligible. Examples: "I'll go see if Moe, Larry, and Curly have made it to the dungeon" (a flight attendant talking about the pilot, copilot, and navigator going to the cockpit); and "Some ankle jerk lost a swervin' Mervin until we raced 'n' maced them" (a police supervisor talking about a foot patrol officer who lost a drunken driver in a high-speed chase).

- Paul Dickson has also written *The Dickson Baseball Dictionary* (Facts on File Inc., 1989), which lists pet words and phrases born from our national sport. For instance, you probably know what a *bullpen* is in baseball, but how about a *buck fifty hitter* or a player who is called a *budder*? (Answers: A buck fifty hitter is one whose batting average is .150, and a *budder* is another word for "rookie.")

- A glossary published by the University of Wisconsin-Extension, entitled *Guide to Nonsexist Language*, documents a special social trend. This booklet is designed to sensitize communicators to commonly used sexist terms. It urges changes in words like manpower, Englishmen, workman, businessman, fireman, manhole, sportsmanship, founding fathers, lady luck, Mother Nature, etc. You get the idea.

The most familiar reference book is, of course, our "standard" dictionary. Each year, there are newspaper articles reporting that a new dictionary is being published with several hundred new words. A recent sampling of these words includes:

- hearing ear dog

- herstory (for women's history)

- white bread (a disparaging term for the white middle class)

- outing (in addition to a "picnic," it is now recognized as "the intentional exposure of a secret homosexual")

- love handles (bulges on the sides of the waist)

*Pity the poor person attempting to learn American English.*

- dissing (showing disrespect for someone or something)
- virus (in computers)
- cow (as in "to have a cow," à la Bart Simpson)
- lambada (the sensual dance)
- slam dancing (another dance; not as sensual)

As one observer stated, "If all these dictionaries and other word reference books were lined up end-to-end . . . we'd deserve it."

New words ooze forth each year unchecked, flowing into libraries and onto bookshelves all over America. Even as you read about them here, new words are being added to the American vocabulary, while others are fading from use.

We now turn to special categories of words that demonstrate the confounding nature of our American language.

## OXYMORONS

*Oxymorons* are pairs of English words that actually contradict themselves. The word itself comes from two Greek words, *oxys* meaning "sharp" or "keen" and *moros* meaning "foolish." Thus, oxymorons are "pointedly foolish" phrases. For example:

Jumbo shrimp (*jumbo* means "large" and *shrimp* usually means something small.) Metal wood (as in a golf club). Evaporated milk. Thunderous silence. Plastic glasses. Leisure activity.

Our nightly TV fare has several oxymorons: guest hosts, epic miniseries, and nightly specials.

Other oxymorons contain more than a dash of sarcasm: military intelligence, airline food, AMTRAK schedule, safe sex, painless dentist, easy payments, and friendly banker.

Oxymorons occur in serious discussions every day. Senator Ted Kennedy accused some of his Republican opponents of staging a *transparent coverup*. The sports pages talk about baseball or football teams acquiring *restricted free agents*. We have also read about *holy wars* being waged in the Middle East, and someone in Congress proposing a *progressive flat-tax*.

Oxymorons clearly demonstrate that, for nonnative speakers trying to learn our language, American English can be downright contradictory. (For a more complete list of these oxymorons, see page 201.)

## NONEXISTENT WORDS

Consider this further irony: We actually have circumstances in our society, well known to all Americans, for which we do not yet have a proper word label.

Here's an interesting example. Your son or daughter is living with someone of the opposite sex, and they are not married. How do they introduce one another? The words *friend, sweetheart,* or *roommate* are inappropriate because they have all been used for decades to describe other circumstances and relationships.

I often ask audiences at my speaking engagements to tell me their solution to this conundrum. Occasionally, someone will speak up and offer *significant other.* That term has gained limited popularity, but we rarely if ever hear a man or woman in a social situation introduce someone as "I'd like you to meet my significant other."

In one of my audiences someone shouted "You call them er-ahs." When I said I didn't understand that term, the respondent explained: "When you introduce them you say, 'I'd like you to meet my . . . errr . . . ahh . . .'" Another respondent offered this euphemism as an appropriate term: *shack-in-law.*

In the 1980 U.S. census, the federal government tried to resolve this omission in our language by inventing the acronym POSSLQ, pronounced *possel-cue.* Government officials wanted to recognize the special state of unmarriedness, so POSSLQ represented "Person of the Opposite Sex Sharing Living Quarters." But, after fifteen years, we rarely (if ever) hear someone introduced as, "This is my POSSLQ."

On one occasion, I said to a bright audience of one hundred company presidents and their spouses, "Let's create the proper term here and now. What do *you* call the person living with your son or daughter when they are not married?" A woman in the back row jumped up and shouted, "That's easy. I call him that son-of-a-bitch!"

## REGIONAL AMERICAN ENGLISH

If you think you speak standard American, think again. Odds are your vocabulary is sprinkled with words peculiar to the region where you spent your adolescence. For example, some of us call a source for public drinking water a *drinking fountain;* others may call it a *bubbler.* Is Coca-Cola or Pepsi a *soda* or *pop?* Or maybe you call *white soda* by another name, *seltzer.* Another example: What do you call those little candies they sprinkle on your ice cream cone? *Sprinkles? Bugs? Jimmies?*

Minor nuances in the language, you say? Don't tell that to Frederic Cassidy, an eminent scholar of English at the University of Wisconsin. For over a decade, he and his team of researchers have been compiling a ponderous reference called the *Dictionary of American Regional English,* or DARE for short. Volume I, published in 1985, contains only words from A through C. It then took the team seven years to publish Volume II. That volume extends only to the letter *H,* but it contains 11,600 head words, 4,975 "additional senses," and some 600 maps.

Cassidy, now in his eighties and a professor emeritus in the English Department at the University of Wisconsin, first proposed this one-of-a-kind dictionary in 1963. He and his researchers have scoured the fifty states asking hundreds of questions at each stop. Samples: "What do you call the time in the early morning before the sun comes into sight?" "What do you call the tallest part on a church building?" "Complete this phrase—I wouldn't know him from _____."

Cassidy and his word sleuths have found that television has not necessarily created a homogeneous melding of our language. This is because you don't communicate with your TV set. Regional words tend to be about everyday things (e.g., rarely do TV newsmen Dan Rather and Peter Jennings talk about paper bags—or *sacks* or *pokes,* as they may be called in certain regions).

## PRONUNCIATION

There are also significant differences in regional pronunciations. The differences between a Brooklyn or New York accent and a southern drawl are obvious even to a neophyte in American English; the laconic twang of the midwesterner is distinctly different from the seemingly lazy extrusions of a Texan.

Foreigners learning American English also have special difficulties with contractions—that's where we shorten words by omitting or combining letters or sounds. For example, shortening *is not* to *isn't*. Combine that difficult grammatical habit with poor pronunciation, and students of American English can go completely mad.

"I cudda proposed that bill to Congress, but it dudn't have a chance until y'all get the facts in order" (President Bill Clinton).

Other common infractions of pronunciation include omitting the first *r* in *library* and *February*, turning the verb *going to* into *gonna*, and dropping that final *g* from just about any verb ending in *-ing*.

A student from Brazil cornered me after one of my lectures and declared that the contraction that vexed him the most was *s'pose*, as in "I s'pose they'll get married eventually."

Anglo-American PR executive Ian Kerr has often questioned our fickleness when pronouncing the names of certain states in the United States. For example, he points out: "Louisiana is pronounced *Looze-iana* by residents there. And Missouri comes out as *Miz-oorah*. But what really baffles me is why Arkansas is called *Ar-kan-saw* when Kansas is pronounced with the final *s-a-s* fully intact."

Perhaps the best example of the baffling inconsistency of pronunciation and spelling in our language is demonstrated in the word *ghoti*. George Bernard Shaw, in his crusade to simplify the English language, conceived this word, saying that a new student of English might logically pronounce *ghoti* as *fish*. How so? The answer: Pronounce the *gh* as in *enough*; pronounce the letter *o* as in *women*; and, finally, pronounce the *ti* as in *nation*. The result? *Fish*.

*I know, teacher. That word is "fish."*

## FILLERS

*Fillers* and *bridges,* the sounds or all-purpose words that we use while searching for a word or collecting our thoughts, are another potential source of confusion for nonnative speakers of American English.

In American English, the best examples of fillers are *um* and *er.* Other American English bridge words are *well* . . . and *anyway* . . . and, the most common of all, *you know.* These are called *vocalized pauses.* They are used by speakers when hesitating, and they signal to the listener that the speaker plans to continue. According to researchers, Americans may use *um* as often as ten or fifteen times a minute and as many as 1,000 times an hour. Ironically, many people don't realize they are saying it.

Vocalized pauses exist in other languages as well, according to *National Geographic* writer Joy Aschenbach, but in decidedly different forms. In Russian, the most common filler appears to be *znachit*. It means . . . well, it means just that: "It means." Russians also use *vot* or *v obshem* as fillers. Germans say *oder* or *nicht*. The Spanish say *este*, which is also the word for "this."

In Japanese, *nah* is used as a pause in a language that may have long pauses. Also, Japanese listeners may frequently utter the word *hai* (which sounds like *hi* and means "yes"). However, *hai* does not necessarily signal agreement. It means "I hear you." This occurs because the Japanese dislike saying no. The reason is that anything that is negative tends to disrupt harmony, which is a cultural taboo among the Japanese.

The British can be heard issuing what might be called a "listening noise," which signals they are hearing you, but not necessarily agreeing. It sounds like a drawn out *MMMmmm*.

One American bridge word that must be especially confusing to non-Americans is probably the most popular and most often uttered word of our teenagers. It's the word *like*. How confusing it must be to hear this: "Like, I really am into rap, you know? It's, like, well, a statement on society. Listen, like, really listen, and, well, like, you'll see for yourself."

## BLACK ENGLISH

Another trend within the American language is what linguists call "black" English versus "white" English. This, of course, refers to the existence, largely denied until the mid-1960s, of a special vernacular developed and spoken by the African-American community.

While black English has added to the richness of the American language stew, William Labov, a linguist at the University of Pennsylvania, calls this increasing separation "dangerous" because it accentuates prejudice and misunderstanding.

Even the preferred label for African-Americans has been evolving: from Negro to colored to black and now to African-American. (Ironically, the lead advocate organization for African-Americans is still called the NAACP—National Association for the Advancement of Colored People.)

## YOUTH SLANG

A linguistic dichotomy of another sort surely exists between generations in America. Slang originated by our youth is not only unique but pervasive and long lasting. The following are excerpts from one glossary published in 1983. Most of these words have woven their way into daily use by persons of all ages.

awesome: outstanding, cool, neat, etc.

bad: something good

bummer: bad news

cool: having style

chill out: calm down

catch some Zs: sleep

hyper: a person who is frenetic

like: used in place of *um*, to fill space

nerd: a wimp, loser, or turkey

rad: radical, outrageous

scope out: to examine

wicked: something great

Within that same 1983 glossary, however, were other bits of slang that failed the test of time. A few examples:

boned: receive a bad grade

coffee: used as a verb, to have breakfast

ex-o: excellent

jag: annoy or bother

Mickey D's: McDonald's

powertool: someone who studies diligently

technicolor yawn: vomit

## POLITICAL JARGON

Another form of regional "speak" comes from that gushing fountain-head of words, our nation's capital, Washington, D.C. For example, in 1993, a new word—*wonk*—leaped into popularity and even spawned its own "wonkspeak." A wonk is a person who is a devoted, even rabid fan or a maven in some particular specialty. Thus, government policy brains or intellectuals are called *wonks.*

Examples of wonkspeak include infrastructure, negative employment growth, incent and incented (used as verbs), green fees (fees intended to keep the planet green), micro-management, and appropriate judgmental standards—a mouthful that means "good rules."

## DOUBLESPEAK

William Lutz teaches in the English Department at Rutgers University and has gained national attention, first, as chairman of the Committee on Public Doublespeak, and, second, as the author of the delightful best-selling book *Doublespeak* (HarperPerennial, 1989). Lutz also serves as editor of the *Quarterly Review of Doublespeak.* That publication and the Committee on Public Doublespeak are creations of the National Council of Teachers of English.

*Doublespeak* is " . . . not a slip of the tongue, or language used out of ignorance, but is instead a very conscious use of language as a weapon or tool by those in power to achieve their ends at our expense," Lutz writes in the introduction to his book. He adds, "While some doublespeak is funny, much of it is frightening . . . The U.S. Army doesn't kill the enemy anymore," says Lutz, "it just *services the target.*" In this same vein, people don't rob automated teller machines; they make *unauthorized withdrawals.* Poor people are *fiscal underachievers.*

Here are some less toxic examples:

- The candy counter in a Madison, Wisconsin, theater is now called the *patron assistance center.*

- A bathroom plunger (sometimes called a *plumber's helper*) is called a *hydroforce blast cup* by the company that makes them.

- Welfare applicants in Maryland no longer meet with clerks. There they are meeting with *eligibility technicians*.

- Boycotts are called *selective buying campaigns*. (And, is there such a thing as a *girlcott?*)

- Bill collectors are called *credit analysts*.

- Tour guides are *destination advisers*.

- Cemeteries now advertise *pre-need arrangements*.

- Policy wonks call a tax hike a *revenue enhancement* or a *tax base erosion control*.

- When former President Carter had his briefing book stolen, the U.S. Justice Department referred to it as *the transfer* of the book.

- Students in Arkansas are no longer *flunked*—instead, they are given *nonpassing grades*.

## BUREAUCRATESE

Government worker Phil Broughton read and heard so many bureaucratic words in his long tenure that he suspected they were often being used without full knowledge of what they meant. He collected the words repeated most often and then, as a demonstration game, grouped them into three columns, as follows:

| | | |
|---|---|---|
| 0. integrated | 0. management | 0. options |
| 1. total | 1. organizational | 1. flexibility |
| 2. systematized | 2. monitored | 2. capability |
| 3. parallel | 3. reciprocal | 3. mobility |
| 4. functional | 4. digital | 4. programming |
| 5. responsive | 5. logistical | 5. concept |
| 6. optional | 6. transitional | 6. time phase |

| 7. synchronized | 7. incremental | 7. projection |
| 8. compatible | 8. third-generation | 8. hardware |
| 9. balanced | 9. policy | 9. contingency |

Here's how to play the game: Select any three numbers. Take the corresponding word from each column, moving from left to right across the three columns, to make a phrase. Work this phrase into your conversation or memo writing. See if anyone questions it. The odds are no one will.

## SUMMARY

Linguists tell us that all languages are complicated. Some have elements that English English and American English do not have. For example, in Spanish, French, and other such popular languages, each noun has a gender—that is, it is either a masculine word or feminine word, with no special logic as to why. For instance, in Spanish, the word for "pulse" is *pulso* and is classified as masculine. But its related word, *pulsacion*, meaning "pulsation," is feminine. Nor does English have the subtle sound inflections of Chinese or the extremely complex grammar of, say, Finnish.

But because English is the predominant language in international business, tourism, and many other more specialized fields, it is heavily laced with a head-spinning collection of unique slang, jargon, buzz words, idioms, allusions, and bureaucratese. These seemingly endless permutations and distortions have created a rich and ever-evolving language capable of adapting to almost any situation. But they have also created a problem: namely, for those born and raised outside the United States, and even for Americans themselves, American English is often terribly confounding.

# 3

# Mangled Misstatements

This chapter has two purposes: first, to demonstrate that American English can often take common sense and kick it around like an empty can on a deserted street; and, second, to *amuse* you. Accordingly, what follows is a collection of actual quotes, inadvertencies, and linguistic nonsense.

Incidentally, the phrase *mangled misstatement* may seem redundant, but it can be explained as follows. A *misstatement* is, obviously, a statement that is wrong or false or that flies against logic. A *mangled misstatement* not only is wrong, but it may also be twisted, pretzel-style, as well. We've all made them. They're the kind that after you've said them, you think, Oh! Wait a minute . . . what I meant to say was. . . . As you read the selections that follow (culled from news reports and other published materials collected over the years), try to imagine how a student of textbook English, or an English-speaking person from another part of the world, would make sense of them. The objective is to prove that, even in our own country, communication is a daily challenge. It's easy to make mistakes, even when using our own brand of lingo.

Del Harris, former head coach of the Milwaukee Bucks basketball team:

I think we have a pretty good basketball team. And we're going to get better as we improve.

**"  "**

A child praying:

Our father who art in heaven, Howard be thy name.

**"  "**

Ed Wold, a former sales manager, had the habit of mixing up his adages. For example, when addressing his salespeople, he would pound the table and say:

A bird in hand grows no moss.

**"  "**

Warren Knowles, the late governor of the state of Wisconsin, had a collection of malapropisms. Here are some of them:

- Senator Coller: "When I started in talking, I was for the bill; but the longer I talked, the more I know I'm against it."

- Supervisor Warnimont: "Milwaukee is the golden egg that the rest of the state wants to milk."

- Senator Tremain: "I'm in favor of letting the status quo stay as it is."

- Senator Zabroski: "Mentally, this shakes me to my very foundation."

- Senator LaFave: "I could go on and excite many other instances of immorality in this withholding."

- Senator Sussman: "By the way, before I start talking, I want to say. . . ."
- Unknown: "I have no political affliction at this time"; "I misquoted myself"; and "I can tell you stories that will make your head stand on end."

**" "**

Casey Stengel:

Well, they tell me it can't be done, but sometimes it doesn't always work.

**" "**

Casey's comment about a fashionable restaurant:

Nobody goes there anymore. It's too crowded.

**" "**

Former President Gerald Ford:

If Lincoln were alive today, he'd roll over in his grave.

Things are more like they are now than they have ever been.

**" "**

Toronto Maple Leaf Coach Frank Smith:

I have nothing to say, and I'm only going to say it once.

**" "**

Albert Hall, onetime assistant secretary of defense:

Well, you know how it is: Nobody's human.

**" "**

From the philosopher/pundit/actress Brooke Shields:

Smoking kills. If you're killed, you've lost a very important part of your life.

**" "**

Columnist James Evans reports that when a doctor instructed a patient to "breathe in and out," she hesitated and finally said, "How else can I breathe?"

**" "**

Then there is the oft told story of the man who approached a public bathroom and was greeted with the sign: "Toilet out of order. Please use floor below." So he did.

**" "**

Former Michigan Governor George Romney:

I didn't say that I didn't say it. I said that I didn't say that I said it. I want to make that very clear.

**" "**

Actor Dennis Hopper:

After the eighties, the nineties will make the fifties look like the sixties.

**" "**

Former Vice President Dan Quayle, attempting to paraphrase the slogan of the United Negro College Fund (A Mind Is a Terrible Thing to Waste), came up with this convoluted version:

What a waste it is to lose one's mind, or not to have a mind is very wasteful. How true that is.

**"    "**

The following statements have been culled from the hallowed halls of state legislatures across the country:

I smell a rat and I intend to nip it in the bud.

It's time to grab the bull by the tail and look it squarely in the eye.

If it weren't for the Rural Electric Associations, we farmers would be watching television by candlelight.

Let's not beat a dead horse to death.

There comes a time to put principles aside and do what's right.

Now we've got them right where they want us.

It's time to swallow the bullet.

My colleague is listening with a forked ear.

This body is becoming entirely too laxative about some matters.

**"    "**

Job application forms are wonderful sources of misstatements. On every application form, there is a section headed *Describe last job duties.* Here are a few responses collected over the past decade:

One applicant who had been a salesclerk in a previous job wrote *sales cluck.*

Another applicant had been a carpenter but wrote *crapender.*

Still another applicant had run a forklift in a warehouse but wrote *had run a frocklift in the whorehouse.*

**" "**

Yogi Berra:

You can observe a lot by watching.

**" "**

A kindergarten teacher asked the class which Christmas story they would like to hear. One boy shouted out, "Tell that one where the father saw Santa Claus and then got sick." Mystified, the teacher kept probing and finally determined that the boy wanted to hear *'Twas the Night before Christmas* and that the child was remembering the part where the father "flew to the window and threw up the sash."

**" "**

Clifford Lord, former director of the Wisconsin State Historical Society, when addressing the annual meeting of the society, *intended* to begin by saying, "It's nice to see so many good friends and familiar faces again." Instead, he muddled his phrases and said, "It's nice to see so many familiar friends and old faces again."

**" "**

Ross and Kathryn Petras have written *The 776 Stupidest Things Ever Said* (Doubleday, 1993) and filled it with malapropisms, misstatements, and doublespeak. Under the category of Freudian slips (where you actually say what's on your mind but didn't mean to say it), they quote Ronald Reagan. In a speech on U.S. efforts to help the Third World, he said, "The United States has much to offer the third world war." The Petrases note that Reagan "repeated this error nine times in the same speech."

**" "**

In the category of things you wish you hadn't said, I was once a guest speaker on a fancy cruise liner. Before my program, a man asked, "What do you speak about?" My answer was, "Well, I speak about idiosyncrasies . . . the crazy things we do . . . you know, quirks." Then, glancing at the man's name tag, I read the man's name: James Quirk.

**" "**

Baseball great Ralph Kiner appears to be perpetuating Yogi Berra's proclivity for the *mal mot*. Kiner, who serves as the broadcaster for the New York Mets, is quoted as saying "We'll be back with the recap after this message."

**" "**

Newspapers are frequent sources for typographical errors that produce totally new meanings; for example:

From a Wisconsin newspaper: "Charlotte G_____, 37, suffered the loss of the tip of the third finger on the right hand when she fell from a moving taxicab Friday night, police reported. G_____ was shitting in the back seat of the cab and had been learning forward conversing with another passenger in the front seat."

**" "**

Newspaper editors will quickly admit that they are not immune from embarrassing inadvertencies. Here is a sampling of actual headlines from news stories, as supplied by Marshall Johnston, former newspaper executive, now retired:

"French Offer Terrorist Reward"

"Don't Tie My Hands on Arms, Reagan Asks Radio Audience"

"10% of Students Fail Classes for Truancy"

"N.J. Judge to Rule on Nude Beach"

**" "**

And, finally, this newspaper headline about a state governor who had exercised a record number of line-item vetoes in state budget legislation. The headline writer had written "GOVERNOR'S PEN IS A SWORD." Unfortunately, the space was missing between the words "PEN" and "IS" . . . making a single word that created a whole new image among swords.

**" "**

In the south-central part of Wisconsin, one will find the village of Tiffany, which consists of only three buildings. One of them is a restaurant and meeting place for the residents, mostly farmers, from the nearby area. The restaurant's interior resembles a scene from a Norman Rockwell painting. Several years ago, on the bulletin board adjacent to the public telephone, this message was pinned: "Mel—Your Aunt Emma called and said she didn't know where she was. She wants you to call her."

**" "**

File this true story under "miscommunications."

Bob Collins is an attorney who also is extremely active in community affairs—president of the school board, founder of the local little league, low-handicap golfer, and member of the police and fire commission. His wife Patricia and their young son Daniel were at the post office one day when a man came along, greeted Pat, and then said to Dan, "And who are you, young man?" Dan politely replied, "I'm Bob Collins's son." "Oh, of course," said the man. "Everyone knows Bob."

Later, in the car, Pat turned to Dan and said: "That was very nice what you replied . . . but you should remember that you are your own person. You are Dan Collins. You are an individual, your own personality. Remember that." Dan said he would.

A week later, while walking down the street, a similar incident occurred. A woman greeted Pat and, turning to young Dan, said, "And you must be Bob Collins's son." Dan paused for a few seconds, then looked the lady squarely in the eye and declared: "No, ma'am, I'm not. My mother told me I'm not."

**"    "**

Accident investigators hear the most inventive excuses from drivers. Here is a collection of explanations for auto mishaps:

"Coming home, I drove into the wrong house and collided with a tree I don't have."

"I thought my window was down, but I found out it was up when I put my hand through it."

"I pulled away from the side of the road, glanced at my mother-in-law, and headed over the embankment."

"In my attempt to kill a fly, I drove into a telephone pole."

"An invisible car came out of nowhere, struck my vehicle, and vanished."

"The indirect cause of this accident was a little guy in a small car with a big mouth."

**" "**

Want to test how well someone understands American English and American culture? In past years, one test was this: Did the person understand the witty, wry, and often topical cartoons in the *New Yorker* magazine? Now a new standard has emerged. At a seminar sponsored by the Pacific Asia Travel Association, one panel of experts agreed that a more modern measurement would be this: Does the person understand "The Far Side" cartoons, as drawn by artist Gary Larson?

For example, one of the best-known Larson cartoons shows two deer standing upright in a forest. One of them has a circular target imprinted on his chest, complete with bull's-eye. The other deer comments, "Bummer of a birthmark, Herb."

Check out "The Far Side" cartoons yourself—they require a thorough understanding of the American scene.

**" "**

In 1992, this was taken from a letter to a dead person from the Greenville County (South Carolina) Department of Social Services: "Your food stamps will be stopped effective March 1992, because we received notice that you passed away. May God bless you. You may reapply if there is a change in your circumstances."

**" "**

An obituary in a Peoria, Illinois, newspaper read: "Mr. John _____ was born in Madison, Wisconsin, where he died and later moved to Peoria."

**" "**

TV sportscaster and former pro football player Matt Millen admitted afterwards that he had stretched a bit too far when trying to describe the rear end of 300-pound tackle Tootie Robbins during a telecast. Millen was obviously trying to find a substitute word for *rear* or *butt* and ended up saying, "Robbins has a huge rectum."

**" "**

Finally, these two true stories are misstatements of another kind. They come from the mouths of children—grandchildren, to be specific.

Six-year-old Timmy was given a scooter by his grandparents and wanted to try it out immediately. "OK," said his grandfather, "but put on that safety helmet we bought you." Timmy demurred, "Why? Why do I have to wear that helmet?" "Because you might fall and break your head open," his grandfather explained. Timmy, looking up at his grandfather's bald head, said in all seriousness, "Is that what happened to you?"

Lucy was ten years old, and her brother Jonathan was six. Seated around the dinner table one evening, the family conversation turned to the question, What do you want to be when you grow up? Lucy replied confidently, "I want to be either a nurse or a teacher." Turning to Jonathan, his mother asked, "And what about you? What do you want to be?" Jonathan said with equal confidence, "I want to be either a brain surgeon . . . or an organ donor."

# Part II

# UNDERSTANDING
# WORLD
# ENGLISH

# 4

# English English

During the first winter of a four-year assignment in England, the antiquated central heating system in our rented home sputtered and stopped. I was told it would take one week to obtain spare parts. Thus, my wife, three young children, and I faced the depressing prospect of seven days of damp, bone-chilling British weather. A kindly neighbor, hearing of our plight, offered to loan us a paraffin burner. To me, as an American, paraffin meant the waxy substance used in making candles. But, desperate as I was, I decided even the meager heat afforded by a few candles would be better than nothing. So I hurried to buy some paraffin at the ironmonger store, complimenting myself for knowing that's what they called a hardware store in England. "Oh, we don't carry paraffin here, sir," was the reply. "You purchase that at the petrol station across the street." Once again, translating that into American, I headed for the nearby gas station. "Yes, we carry paraffin," the attendant confirmed. "But where is your tin?" he asked. I looked at him dumbly. "Tin?" I asked, imagining myself stuffing wax into a tin. "Yes, sir. You'll need a tin. You can purchase one at the ironmongers." Reversing my tracks, I purchased my tin and presented it to the attendant at the petrol station. He then walked to a large metal drum and began pouring kerosene into my tin. It finally dawned on me that in England, paraffin was the word for kerosene. Survival in England, I discovered, was going to mean an everyday conflict with words.

For Americans visiting or living on "that green and lovely island," this example of one fog-filled misunderstanding has undoubtedly been repeated many times.

Our language differences, however, are narrowing, according to some social observers. And the reason is television. Omnivorous TV programming appetites in both countries have caused a flourishing trade between British and American networks. "Masterpiece Theatre," a series of classic British stories, has been a huge hit in the United States, while "Dallas" was a prime-time winner in England. In recent years, the pace of such imports has accelerated to the point where British accents—and British terminology—can be heard in prime time at least weekly on American TV channels.

Television notwithstanding, a vast number of differences still exist in our respective usages of English. Indeed, the British view was dryly expressed in the stage musical and movie *My Fair Lady* with the slam that "Americans haven't spoken English in years."

Underscoring this belief, in 1993, the British Broadcasting Company expressed its distaste over the "contamination" of the Queen's English by Uncle Sam with a directive to its staff to avoid the incursion of Americanisms—such things as *chairwoman* and *chairperson*, and attaching the suffix *gate* to every British scandal (a la Washington's *Watergate*). In rebuttal, public television commentator Robert MacNeil (and coauthor of *The Story of English*) commented: "What many Brits don't realize is that the rest of us in the English-speaking world now far outnumber them. America is driving the language now [and] Americans are in every way greater innovators [than the British, whose] imperial condescension has been superseded by a cultural inferiority complex."

Or, to use American slang: "In your face!"

Americans frequenting the United Kingdom on business, or as students or tourists, invariably return with stories about "crazy" terms and embarrassing mix-ups involving misunderstood British words, phrases, and even traditional symbols. Here are some examples:

"Custom" tailoring is called *bespoke* in England. Why? And why do the British end sentences with a *full stop* instead of a "period"? And how did a "trailer truck" on U.S. "highways" become an *articulated lorry* on British *motor-*

*ways?* Finally, when it comes to symbols, any American knows that it is bad luck to have a black cat cross one's path. Not so in England. In fact, there just the opposite is true. A black cat, it is believed, will bring *good* luck.

In this short chapter, we cannot list all of the differences between English English and American English usages and beliefs. However, a careful search of your neighborhood library or book store will turn up numerous dictionaries and reference books devoted solely to inventorying contrasting American and English words. At the conclusion of this chapter, you will find the titles of four such books that I have found both readable and informative. Instead of reproducing lists of mind-numbing word comparisons and differences, this chapter offers a selection of examples to allow you to become more aware of the problem.

We begin with a few seemingly innocent words that might shock the *knickers* (English for "panties") off your British counterparts.

## BLOODY AWFUL WORDS

First off, the singular British expression *bloody* is not as crude as many Americans believe. It could be compared with the American slang word *darn*, and can be heard coming from most British, regardless of social level. Incidentally, there are two supposed origins for this phrase: first, that it is a slang contraction of *by our lady*; and second, that it is a vestige from the reign of Mary, Queen of Scots, who was known as *Bloody Mary* because of her short but violent monarchy in the sixteenth century.

While *bloody* is fairly benign in Great Britain, consider this list of seemingly innocent words—innocent, at least, to American ears but startling stuff to the British:

| | |
|---|---|
| stuffed | fanny |
| randy | buggered |
| sharp | vest |
| napkins | on the job |

Ready for your ears to burn? If so, here are the unadulterated British meanings for each of the aforementioned words.

*stuffed:* Vulgar slang for "having sex with a woman"; or if used as *Get stuffed!* it means "go to hell!" Another bit of slang meaning "to engage in sex" is *to bonk.*

*fanny:* In England, this does not refer to a person's derriere, but instead to a female's genitalia. Similarly, a *willy* is, for an Englishman, his penis.

*randy:* This is not the familiar form of the name Randolph; in England, it is synonymous with our word *horny.*

*buggered:* An American might say, "I'll be buggered," meaning confused or confounded; or we might refer to a cute child or animal as a *cute little bugger.* But in England, *to be buggered* is to commit sodomy. In English business lingo, the *buggeration factor* is akin to Murphy's Law (i.e., "What can go wrong usually does.")

*sharp:* If an American describes a colleague as *sharp,* it is a compliment, meaning the person is quick, intelligent, and able; but in England, it means the person is devious and unprincipled.

*vest:* What an American calls a *vest* is known as a *waistcoat* to an English person; a *vest* in England is an undershirt, so Americans should be wary of admiring an Englishman's vest.

*napkins:* In England, *napkins* are "diapers," also referred to as *nappies;* a table napkin in England is called a *serviette.*

*on the job:* In England, this is a slang expression for "having sex," which explains why one British gentleman expressed delight when an American acquaintance casually mentioned that his father "was eighty years old when he died on the job."

Now, here is a list of decidedly "blue" words in our American dialect—words that are vulgar and perk up sensitive ears in the United States, but are perfectly innocent when used by the British:

*Innocent British words mean entirely different things to Americans.*

| | | |
|---|---|---|
| pecker | bangers | to knock up |
| rubber | pissed | scheme |
| cheap | homely | to bomb |
| vet | tinkle | spotted dick |

Here are the definitions for those words as used in Great Britain:

*Pecker* refers to the chin; so don't be surprised if a Britisher says to you, in an attempt to perk up your spirits, "Keep your pecker up."

*Bangers* are sausages in Great Britain, which means you might easily hear a pub patron order "a beer and a banger, please."

*To knock up* can be used with complete impunity in several ways in England: it can mean "to wake me up" on the telephone, or, in the game of tennis, it can mean rallying the ball back and forth in practice before starting a game. (Note: On my first trip to England, I was invited to play tennis with a charming young lass who coolly inquired, "Would you like to knock up first?")

*Rubber* is the word for "erasers"; therefore, you can understand why Florida PR executive Gary Stogner was so shocked on hearing an English architect friend cry out, "Who nicked my rubber? It was my favorite rubber. I had it for over three years!" Later, Stogner deciphered his friend's complaint to mean "Who *stole* my *eraser?*"

*Pissed* is not an expression of anger, as it is in the United States; in England, it usually means someone is very drunk.

*Scheme,* for most Americans, is a negative word, because we consider a scheme something that is a bit sly and slick; in England, however, it is just a synonym for the word *plan.*

*Cheap,* for Americans, connotes something of poor quality; in England, however, it is used more often to refer to something inexpensive, as in a *cheap day ticket* on the railroad.

*Homely* does not mean unattractive in England; rather, it is just the opposite—a person in England who is homely is "home-like," meaning a warm and comfortable person.

*To bomb* means "to succeed," rather than the American connotation, which means "to fail." So, in England, if something is described as *It went like a bomb,* it means that it was a large triumph.

*Vet* does not refer to a veterinarian; but, instead, it is used as a verb and means "to thoroughly check something over," as in the phrase *Let me vet your proposal before we send it.*

*Tinkle* is used as in the statement *Give me a tinkle,* which means to phone someone, or as the British would say, "I will ring you tomorrow."

*Spotted dick* is a pudding, and the "spots" are ordinary raisins; you'll find this unique dessert listed frequently on English menus.

## RIDING THE HIGHWAY OF WORDS

When it comes to word differences, the roadways of our respective countries are filled with varied verbal traffic.

Driving on the left side of the road is not the only oddity Americans encounter when getting behind the wheel in the United Kingdom. In a British automobile, there are some *sixty* differences in the terminology for various parts of an auto. An American car has a hood, but the same car in England has a *bonnet*. Similarly, the dashboard is, in Britain, the *fascia panel*. Our windshield is their *windscreen*. The trunk is the *boot*, the fender is the *wing*, and the muffler is the *exhaust silencer*. Even the so-called driver's side and passenger side of a car, as we call them in the United States, are translated differently. In England, the right side of a car, opposite the sidewalk, is the *offside*, and the left side is the *nearside*.

As for the roads themselves, in England, *motorways* are what we would call expressways. Also, *highways* in England are main, well-traveled roads, and *byways* are the less-traveled, winding, and always picturesque back roads.

Center lines on British roads are marked with *cat's-eyes*. These refer to a pair of reflector studs set at close intervals into road surfaces that, at night, clearly mark the center of the road. The official word for them is *studs*, which explains why a driver might occasionally see a sign along a British highway advising *No studs for 2 miles*.

In the United States, we do not have many English-style *round-abouts*, which are where two roads meet. But in the United Kingdom, roundabouts are possibly more common than our conventional intersections with stoplights. Roundabouts are what we might describe as "intersections with circular islands in the center." This causes traffic to feed clockwise into the circular flow of traffic and then to leave the circle at the desired exit. (Note: During my tour in England, I once overheard the comment, "Well, what you lose on the swings, you gain on the roundabouts." This is the equivalent of our phrase *Six of one and half a dozen of the other*. I interpreted the British phrase to mean "What you lose on the swings (of the roads) you gain on the roundabouts (or circles of traffic)." I was wrong. In this case, that phrase refers to the swings and roundabouts found on a *playground*; roundabouts on a British playground are what we would call *merry-go-rounds*.)

Our curbs are spelled as *kerbs* in England, and our tires are spelled as *tyres*; however, they refer to the same thing. Rest areas are called *lay-bys*. Exit roads are labeled *Way Out*, which too often prompts some Americans to comment, "Oh, that's waaaay out, man!" Parking lots in England are called *car parks*, and the grassy areas along a main highway in England are called *verges*.

To power your auto, you need *petrol*, although the word *gasoline* is understood perfectly. Petrol is *dear*, or "expensive" in England; it won't seem that way at first, however, because the British have switched to the metric system and petrol is now sold and measured in liters, which contain slightly more than a quart.

Finally, if you should happen to hear a Britisher boast that he or she *did a ton* during a motor trip, it means he or she hit or exceeded the 100-mile-an-hour mark.

## FOOD IS NOT NECESSARILY FOODE

One stereotype of England is that to make something quaint and "veddy" British, one need only add an *e* to a word. For example: Ye Olde Antique Shoppe. Even though *foode* is not one of these, there are several differences in the food category worth noting.

Let's start with *bubble and squeak*. In truth, this is just another word for casserole. It originates from the English custom of having a proper midday meal each Sunday, where the main fare is usually *a joint*, meaning a roast or joint of meat, such as lamb. Then the leftover meat plus the leftover vegetables and potatoes can be saved and mixed for the Monday meal. When heated in the oven, as the various juices and flavors fuse together, this mixture issues little bubbles and squeaks.

Order a filet of beef in England and the word *filet* is usually pronounced with a hard *t* sound, unlike the French pronunciation (which Americans use) where the *t* is silent.

What Americans call french fries are *chips* in England. And to add further confusion, what we call potato chips in the United States are called *crisps* in England.

An American hot dog is a *frank* to a Britisher. *Lolly* means "candy" (but it can also mean "money"), and *jelly* refers to "Jell-o" not "jam."

To have tea in England often means more than sipping a hot brew. First, tea is usually served with *biscuits* on the side. Hearing this, Americans would probably envision a type of roll, perhaps a baking powder biscuit. But biscuits in England are what Americans call *cookies.* Also, Americans should refrain from ordering "cheese and crackers." Crackers are toys that are distributed at English birthday and Christmas parties, the ones where you pull two tabs outward in opposite directions and they create a loud popping sound. *High tea* is served late in the afternoon and involves more food than just cookies. Among the working class, the evening meal may be called *tea.*

According to the *New York Times*, the *power tea* has replaced the business *power lunch* in Britain. It seems the fad now, especially in London, is to conduct business discussions later in the day over tea and scones rather than at midday over, say, dover sole, two vegetables, and wine. Americans, especially on the East Coast, are borrowing this trend.

On dessert menus, you will see the word *flan*, which is a soft pielike pudding, often in a bit of pastry.

Also, if someone offers you *gammon,* it is just another term for a thick piece of ham.

In Scotland, *haggis* is considered the national dish. You should know that its main ingredient is the entrails of a sheep, and when served, it has the appearance of hash.

Some other regional differences: *Yorkshire pudding* is actually puffs of batter baked in roast beef juices, and *Cornish pasties* from the county of Cornwall are meat-and-vegetable-filled pastries.

Other translations: *Sultanas* are golden raisins; *neaps* are turnips; *cockie leekie* is a thick soup made with chicken stewed in prunes and leeks; and *wow-wow sauce* is a sauce made with meat stock that, incidentally, goes well with *bubble and squeak.*

If you visit a typical English pub (often called *the local* by frequent patrons), you should learn this short glossary:

*Bitter* refers to the popular beer drunk in England, which, contrary to American belief, is *not* served warm; it is, however, served at room temperature, which, in England, will be cool but not ice cold.

*Lager* is also beer, but it is a lighter colored and more carbonated beer, similar to the popular American brands.

*Stout* is a heavier, darker form of English beer.

*Whisky* in England means scotch whisky; if you wish bourbon whiskey (note the spelling difference), you must specify that (but it may not be available because it must be imported from the United States and is very expensive).

*Martini* is a popular brand of vermouth; so if you want an American-style martini, specify a *gin martini*.

A *pink gin* is gin with a dash of bitters and perhaps a touch of water.

A *shandy* is a mixture of beer and ginger beer or lemonade.

To order a drink *neat* in England means "no water."

It is also helpful to know that when you see a pub labeled *free house* it means that it is not owned or affiliated with a particular brewery.

## GRAMMAR: GARBLED OR GRAND?

When listening to how words are strung together in England, an American would conclude that rules of grammar, as taught in our high schools, were being severely violated.

For example, people in England do not go to *the* hospital; they *go to hospital* or *go in hospital*. And politicians in United States *run* for office; in England, they *stand* for office.

Another usage that jolts the eardrums of Americans is when verbs and collective nouns do not agree. In England, this applies when speaking of institutions or political bodies. Here are some examples:

| American | British |
|---|---|
| Notre Dame plays Michigan. | Oxford play Cambridge. |
| The U.S. Congress adjourns. | The House of Commons rise. |
| General Motors has declared a dividend. | Rolls Royce have canceled their dividend. |

Thus, where words like *committee* and *government* take singular verbs in American English, they take plural verbs in England; for example, *The committee were. . . .* and *The government are. . . .*

The English also love the word *got*, as in *The game got played.* But in the United States, the preference is to avoid *got* and use the more standard verb *was.*

Another common trait in England is to make a statement in the form of a question but absent the rising inflection. For example, *It's not too difficult, is it?* or, *It's not raining hard, is it, really?*

## SPELLING

Differences in spelling also abound. Here are just a few examples:

| American | British |
|---|---|
| color | colour |
| honor | honour |
| center | centre |
| jewelry | jewellery |
| traveling | travelling |
| skeptical | sceptical |
| aluminum | aluminium |
| inflection | inflexion |
| check | cheque |
| jail | gaol |
| whisky | whiskey |

| maneuver | manoeuvre |
| license  | licence   |
| practice | practise  |

## IS IT *BRITON* OR *BRIT?*

An "alien," English writer George Mikes advises, may become British but never English. Or, stated another way, many can be British but few can be English.

To explain that riddle, Mikes is claiming that being British can mean being a naturalized subject of Great Britain; but being English means English in culture, outlook, heart, and spirit.

The word *Briton*, Mikes offers, sounds historical or literary and, of course, derives from the region of Brittany, which first belonged to England and then France. As for the word *Britisher*, it sounds like an Americanism, but the key to remember is that it is more polite and proper than the unflattering, ugly sounding, and abrupt word *Brit*.

If one understands the geography of the country, other labels become easier to understand. The entire triangular-shaped island is properly called *Great Britain* and consists of three individual but united countries: England, Scotland, and Wales. Cross the Irish Sea and throw in Northern Ireland, and the result is called the *United Kingdom*, or *U.K.*

As for the differences between *Scots*, *Scotch*, *Scottish*, and *Scotland*, here is the explanation: the people who live in Scotland are Scots who drink Scotch, and tartans are Scottish. Also, a *plaid* is not a pattern but an item of clothing.

And why are the British called *Limeys?* The answer is that in past centuries sailors were frequent sufferers of scurvy until it was discovered that they could be protected by citrus fruits. Since the British were renowned seafarers, the British became known as *Limeys*, from the lime juice rations given to sailors.

## A DOG'S BREAKFAST

In England, *a dog's breakfast* is a phrase used to denote any kind of conglomeration or mishmash. It derives from the practice where leftover food from a dinner is saved and dumped into the dog's food bowl. So, it seems appropriate to finish this chapter with a dog's breakfast of Englishisms—a collection of bits and pieces that will broaden your awareness of English English.

Let's start at the *first floor*. In England, that's what Americans would call the *second floor*. Reason: In England, the first floor is called the *ground floor*, which then, logically, makes the next floor the *first floor*. And if you choose to take the elevator to the first floor, look for the *lift*.

Even the day's weather is viewed from different sets of eyes. Where an American encounters a very light rain, an Englishman is likely to say, "Oh, it's just spitting a bit." And a steady downpour in New York is likely to be described as "raining hard enough to settle the dust" in London.

As for contrasting perceptions of temperatures, Alistair Cooke, the great chronicler of differences between America and the United Kingdom, puts it this way: "In England, I have seen newspaper headlines that read 'Temperature Expected to Hit 75 Degrees Again Today—No Relief in Sight.'" Consequently, Cooke explains that a *light suit* to a Britisher means "light colored"; whereas to an American, it means "light weight."

Turning to more mundane differences, a baby's pacifier is called a *dummy*, and a baby's carriage is called a *pram*.

Anything that is referred to as *dodgy* or *dicey* means it is risky or a bit delicate, perhaps even in a legal way.

*Flexes* and *points* are the words used for electrical wires and outlets in England.

If you want to rent something (such as a car or TV set, but not a dwelling) in England, you *hire* it. And to buy something on the installment plan, is to buy via *hire purchase* or, as it is called colloquially, *the never-never plan*.

A master of ceremonies is called a *compere,* and a *pantomime* is a traditional form of musical entertainment for children at Christmas and is usually based on a famous nursery rhyme. Also, what Americans might call a magician is called a *conjurer.* And if you go to a village fair, it is called a *fete.*

An inexpensive ballpoint pen is called a *biro* (pronounced *by-row*) and originates from the name of its inventor, a Czech named Lazlo Biro.

Perhaps you've wondered where the popular British exclamation *blimey* comes from. The answer is that it's a contraction from the longer exclamation *God blind me!*

Police officers are called *bobbies* because the first national police force in England was founded by Sir Robert Peel in 1829.

If you're visiting England and need to find a drugstore, it is called a *chemist.* And if you wish to inquire whether a specific category of goods (such as pens or kitchenware) is carried in a large department store, you should say "Do you *do* pens (or kitchenware)?"

*Santa Claus* is a known term, but in England he is also called *Father Christmas.* (Note: Thanksgiving is a decidedly American term and holiday, although one British wag once said to me sarcastically, "I suppose you could say we celebrate Thanksgiving on the Fourth of July.")

A *nipple* refers only to the nipple on a woman's breast and not to the rubber-type nipple on an American baby bottle. That, in England, is called a teat.

If an English person refers to you using any of the following terms, you should take offense because they are unflattering to say the least.

*twit:* a fool

*toff:* a big shot, a show-off

*pseud:* a fake

*poseur:* artificial, or trying to impress

*sod:* roughly, a bastard

*ass:* a fool—but not as rude as in America, where it refers to a part of the anatomy

*bum:* does not mean a tramp, but much worse — an ass, or the rectum

*bent:* crooked, or homosexual

*berk:* stupid and disagreeable

*a tart:* a cheap, loose woman

*dotty:* crazy, eccentric, as in "He's a bit dotty."

*flibbertigibbet:* a flighty girl, or an impish man

*mug:* a sucker

*nancy:* a homosexual

In England, a *French letter* is not a letter from a Frenchperson. It is the slang for "prophylactic." The French get retribution by referring to prophylactics as *English caps.*

If you wish to go to the bathroom in England, the proper terminology is: *to have a wash* or *to visit the loo.* Other terms include *the men's* or *the ladies* and the WC (for "water closet"). A member of the older generation might wish to *spend a penny,* which derives from the days when a penny was required in the public pay toilets.

An American *backyard* means, to a Britisher, a small paved area where *dustbins* (or "garbage cans") are stored. The entire area behind a Britisher's home with grass and flowers is called *the garden.*

If you work for a British firm, you don't receive *compensation* for your labors; that word is used to refer to retribution for damages, not as pay for your work.

If you walk the streets of any city in England, you'll see For Sale signs on dwellings but with the words *freehold* or *leasehold* added. The former designates ownership of both the dwelling and the land; the latter term indicates only tenancy, but usually for many, many years.

A vacuum cleaner is often referred to as a *hoover,* after that well-known brand of carpet sweepers. A TV set is often called the *telly,* and a refrigerator the *fridge.* If a Britisher is *peckish,* it merely means that he or she should make a trip to the *fridge* because he or she is a bit hungry.

If you should be invited to a party and the invitation reads *fancy dress,* you will be embarrassed if you show up in a tuxedo or long gown. *Fancy dress* in Great Britain means the party will feature costumes.

Another bit of protocol to note is that the English rarely respond to the comment *thank you* with the follow-up phrase *you're welcome*, as Americans do. Instead, the British customarily respond by repeating the words, *thank you.*

If you've ever been curious about Cockney, that unique, almost indecipherable language of those born in the East End of London, I recommend you forget it! That rhyming bit of seemingly nonsensical dialect is truly a language unto its own. For example, the *stairs* are referred to as *apples and pears* simply because *stairs* rhymes with *pears*. Perhaps Eliza Doolittle of *My Fair Lady* fame was smarter than we thought. (Note: For more examples of Cockney, refer to the Glossaries.)

## REFERENCE BOOKS

Four books that I have found to be very useful in recording translations are as follows:

*British/American Language Dictionary*, by Norman Moss (Passport Books, 1984).

*Understanding British English: The Gap between the English Language and Its American Counterpart*, by Margaret E. Moore (Carol Publishing, 1992).

*English English*, by Norman W. Schur (Verbatim, 1980).

Finally, for an amusing survival guide to the differences between British and American thinking, read Jane Walmsley's entertaining and insightful book *Brit-Think Ameri-Think*, (Harrap Books Ltd., 43-45 Annandale St., Edinburgh EH7 4A2, Scotland, first published in 1988 and reprinted in 1992).

These books will equip you with knowledge of thousands of words and meanings from A to Z . . . or, as the British would say, *A* to *Zed.*

Also, the reader who wishes to get a jump start at learning a bit of Brit-speak will find a glossary of common words and their American meanings beginning on page 192. This particular list was compiled by British business executive John McGill who, until his retirement, worked for the American 3M Corporation. McGill reports that he and his wife developed the list "out of self-defense because so many of my American business colleagues assigned to Britain needed a quick dose of translation medicine to help them acclimate."

## SUMMARY

It should now be obvious that serious misunderstandings can result between two so-called English-speaking peoples. And serious is the right word for it. Sir Winston Churchill reported in his chronicles that during World War II, a misunderstanding at a high-level meeting over a single word (the verb *to table*) resulted in what he termed a "long and acrimonious argument." For Americans, *to table* means "to shelve" or "to delay action," whereas to the British, it means precisely the opposite, as in "to lay on the table for immediate consideration."

Here's a final anecdote about the sometimes rocky marriage between English English and American English. And, indeed, this involves a true-life marriage between Britisher Steven Portch, a former vice president at the University of Wisconsin System, and his American wife, Barbara.

> Shortly after they were married, and while living in the United States, Barbara asked Steven to go to the store to buy some buns for supper. What she didn't know was that in England *buns* are not the round rolls we use for hamburgers. Steven dutifully returned with the purchase and, without examining them, Barbara asked Steven to "please slice the buns." Thinking that was a bit strange, Steven did as he was told. Minutes later, Barbara entered the dining room with a plate of cooked hamburgers. "Where are the buns?" she asked. "And why in the world do you have those sweet rolls sliced and on the table?"

Even the British Broadcasting Company's style book could probably not anticipate—or sort out—that muddle!

For Americans, it usually takes a specially tuned ear to identify one from the other. Misidentifying these accents is tantamount to committing a "pedodontric" (foot-in-mouth) *faux pas.* It would be comparable to calling someone from New England a *Rebel* and a Georgian a *Yank.* Those who confuse a South African with an Australian or a New Zealander because of accent put themselves in a *balls-up* situation. (Read that as a "messed up and embarrassing" situation.) Here is an example:

> Cruising aboard the Royal Viking *Sun* in the South China Sea, my wife and I were seated at a dinner table with a charming, distinguished looking couple named Templeton. He had a clipped mustache, she a creamy complexion, and both spoke with strong British accents. My assessment of their nationality was completed when I overheard the maitre d' refer to him as "Sir Reginald." Accordingly, for my opening conversational gambit, I asked, confidently "Where in England do you live?" The slightly cool reply was, "We live in Melbourne . . . Melbourne, that's in Australia."
>
> Moral: Never guess. Rather than err, don't even try an *educated* guess. Better to wait for other clues by asking a few discreet questions. For example, "Where is your home?" which implies that you *know* their country of origin and are merely asking in which city they live, or if they live in the city or the countryside.

We begin this study of the language spoken by our various English-speaking cousins by turning northward to our closest neighbors.

## CANADA

The relationship between the two peoples with the longest, friendliest, most open border in the world—Americans and Canadians—is perhaps best described by a banker from the border city of Buffalo, New York, who said, "I know when I'm in Canada . . . but I just can't prove it."

Indeed, if an American were dropped out of the sky on one side or the other of the Canadian-American border, from the standpoint of language alone, he or she would have difficulty knowing which of the two countries he or she was in. (We'll come to the matter of Quebec in a moment.)

When distinguishing between the speech of a Canadian and that of an American, there are a few clues. The most prominent tip-off is a one-syllable bit of phonetic punctuation used by many English-speaking Canadians. Instead of ending sentences with a downward inflection of the voice, Canadians tend to terminate their sentences with an audible, near grunt that comes out as "Eh?" It is uttered in such a manner that the sentence falls somewhere between a declarative statement and a question. It also seems to invite agreement.

In addition, Canadians tend to pronounce one other particular syllable differently. That is the *ou* sound, as in the words *out, about,* and *house.* Where Americans say those words with an *ow* sound, Canadians prefer the *oo* sound, as in the word *stool.*

Certain word usages differ as well. Canadians take *holidays* where Americans take *vacations.* Americans live in *states,* and Canadians live in *provinces.* A *napkin* to an American is a *serviette* to a Canadian. Where an American's dog might be *lost,* a Canadian's animal *went missing.*

Other word differences: What Americans call a *sofa* may be called a *chesterfield* in Canada. A Canadian student receives *marks,* whereas a U.S. student receives *grades.* People in the United States now refer to American Indians by using the preferred term *Native Americans.* A similar change is occurring in Canada, but there the term of choice for their Native Americans is *First Nations.*

Among Canadians, occasional words have been imported from the mother country; so as you listen to a Canadian, your ear might be jarred by a seemingly out-of-place word. The explanation is that it probably can be traced to English English.

### Canadian Cultural Taboos

While Americans and Canadians fly freely back and forth across the border and therefore may be considered "birds of a feather," there are a few distinct cultural characteristics that identify the two populations.

One of those traits is that Americans are considered "benevolently ignorant" about Canadians. If you doubt that, take this quick test: Name five famous historic Canadian figures. Most Americans have spent little time studying Canadian history, geography, government, or culture. In contrast, Canadians are described as "malevolently well informed" about the United States. They are deluged with information about their neighbor to the south, to the point that many feel overshadowed, even resentful toward Americans.

The gravest cultural insult an American can make is to chauvinistically assume that "Canadians are just like us." Wrong! Canadians are fiercely proud of their special heritage and are offended when people lump them with Americans. Striving to reinforce their individualism, a Canadian magazine once conducted a contest asking readers to complete the sentence *As Canadian as . . . .* The magazine hoped some memorable descriptive phrase would emerge that captured the Canadian ethos, something as unique as *As American as hot dogs, baseball and apple pie.* The winning entry in the contest proved to be *As Canadian as possible, under the circumstances.* (Note: Add a dry sense of humor to the many admirable Canadian qualities.)

### Quebec

Any American living in the North and the East who is anxious to visit the closest, most significantly different cultural enclave, should head directly to the delightful cities of Montreal and Quebec in the province of Quebec. Residents there like to say they were "born under the *fleur de lis,* but raised under the rose." This, of course, refers to the national symbol of France, the lily, and the British Tudor rose.

The French explorer Jacques Cartier started it all. In 1534, he landed in the *baie de Gaspe,* marking the discovery of Canada. In 1608, his countryman Samuel de Champlain established French settlements in what are now the cities of Montreal and Quebec. By 1763, when the British defeated the French in what we call the French and Indian Wars, the French colony numbered only 70,000 people in the midst of some 2 million British. However, that French foothold prevailed, and today French is the official language for the province of Quebec, where 5.4 million consider French their mother tongue, while 1.1 million speak English or another language. Quebec also encourages French-speaking immigrants. Consequently, there has been an influx of emigration from places like Algeria and Haiti.

Differences between the English and French cultures in Canada begin with the very pronunciation of the word *Quebec*. Which is correct: *KAY-bek* or *KWA-bek*? The answer is that the former is the French pronunciation and the latter is the English version. In fact, because of special pride in their ethnic heritage, people from Quebec will often identify themselves first as *KAY-bekers* rather than as *Canadians.*

So zealous are modern-day French nationalists in Quebec that, in 1977, English was banned from *all* signs: billboards, highway signs, retail store fronts, and so on. This law was enforced by official "language police," who sought out and fined sign violators. However, in 1993, bowing to pressure from businesses that cater to English-speaking visitors, an amendment was passed eliminating the police "tongue troopers" and allowing commercial signs to appear in both French and English, as long as the French was "predominantly" larger. Suppression of English in Quebec has been condemned by both the Canadian Supreme Court and the United Nations as a violation of the Canadian Charter of Rights and Freedoms.

In spite of this regional controversy involving Quebec, it is essential that Americans know — and respect — that the *entire* country of Canada is officially bilingual. All government publications and commercial packaging must, by law, be printed in both English and French.

Also, in daily discourse be aware that French is not limited to just Quebec. You will find many Canadians — even those as far away as Vancouver, in the western-most province of British Colombia — fully fluent in French. About one-quarter of Canada's 27 million people consider French their mother tongue.

## AUSTRALIA

G. A. Wilkes, a professor of English literature at Sydney University, claims that "it's fair to say that two Australians could have a conversation that no other English speaker could understand."

As an example, author Helen Jonsen, who wrote *Kangaroo's Comments and Wallaby's Words* (Hippocrene Books, 1988), offers this simple sentence: "Can I bot a chewie?" That's merely Australian English for: "May I borrow a piece of gum."

Aussies love their special brand of coined and abbreviated words, all spoken as if there were no spaces between them. Paul Gigot, writing for the *Wall Street Journal,* says that the Australian name for this dialect is *Strine.* That's how Australians say the word *Australian.* And if they speak Strine, they also refer to themselves as *Aussies,* pronounced as *Ozzies,* with a *z* sound. Consequently, they also say they live in the land of "Oz."

Pronunciation is, indeed, a unique feature of Strine. It certainly isn't British. A few words suggest, perhaps, a Boston accent. To Americans, it also sounds a bit sing-songy with its "wordsallruntogether" and special emphasis on final words and syllables.

Gigot claims Australians can make insults sound like compliments. Take the word *bastard,* for instance. "Aussies use it affectionately," Gigot writes, "as in the phrase 'Cute little bastard, isn't he?'"

As a further example of how those who live "down under" turn phrases upside down, take the term *bugger* or *buggered.* As we pointed out in Chapter 4, in England, this term is terribly rude because it refers to sodomy. In Australia, it is much more benign and simply means "to be exhausted."

It is understandable that Australian English has become so unique. Colonized from England, Australia's first settlers were prisoners sent there for punishment—to the largest island in the world. They were met by the Aborigines, and as a result, London street slang merged with indigenous words for places, plants, and animals never before seen on other continents.

As a result, a visitor will discover specimens of Aussie slang as plentiful as seashells along Australia's endless beaches. George Renwick is a cross-cultural trainer and expert on working with Australians. He writes that "in Australia, much more so than in the United

*An Australian could converse and no other English speaker would understand.*

States, language is a mixture of imaginative metaphor and swearing." He then quotes Australian writer John O'Grady, who describes Australian English as "pungent, succinct, apt, sometimes explosive, frequently profane, and always irreverent."

Note: For a delightful insight into Australians, read Renwick's book *A Fair Go for All, Australian/American Interactions* (Intercultural Press, 1991).

Here are some common terms an American might encounter:

*the ABC, or Aunty:* the Australian Broadcasting Company

*Aussie Rules:* Australian Rules Football, a rough-and-tumble game that mixes elements of American football (but with no protective padding) and English rugby

*banana-bender:* a resident of the state of Queensland

*bangers:* Bangkok, Thailand; or (as in England) sausages

*barmy:* crazy

*bathers:* swimsuit; also called a *cozzie* or *togs*

*billabong:* a pond in an otherwise dry stream

*bickies:* short for biscuits, which (as in England) refer to cookies (and not crackers)

*bloke:* a guy

*brekky:* breakfast

*brolly:* an umbrella

*bugger all:* nothing; as in "There was bugger all to do."

*brumby:* a wild horse

*bushie:* anyone living in the bush; also called a *bushman*

*camp:* gay, or homosexual

*cobber:* a close friend

*cuppa:* a cup of tea

*dag:* a nerd, or even a little worse

*Enzed:* a New Zealander, from the letters N and Z (with the last letter pronounced *zed*)

*fair dinkum:* Something true, genuine; an assertion of truth or genuineness

A glossary with more Strine terms begins on page 181.

Finally, Nino Amato, an economic development executive from Wisconsin, tells of how he was abruptly introduced to this special brand of lingo.

On my first night in Australia, I went to the bar in my hotel, sat down, and ordered a drink. An attractive young lady with a short skirt and plenty of makeup sat down next to me and said, "G'day, Yank. Are you randy?" So I naturally replied, "No. I'm Nino." With a disgusted look, she turned around and walked away. It wasn't until several days later that I learned that the word *randy* in Australia (and England) means *horny*.

## NEW ZEALAND

June Partridge of Auckland works for an American company located in New Zealand. When I asked her what bothered her most about working for an American firm, she quickly replied, "Oh, that's easy. It's when my American boss answers a question by saying 'I suppose so.'" I asked "Why is that so vexing?" She replied, "Because to a New Zealander that's a non-answer. Does it mean yes or no? I always have to ask if that means yes or no."

Later, I commented that if I included her little piece of information in this book I would try to remember to send her a complimentary copy. With a friendly smile, she replied, "Don't worry. If I don't receive one, I'll chase you up." (Another non-American phrase—and memorable to the point that you can be certain I'll send her that book promptly, to avoid being *chased up*.)

I once spent an evening with a pair of warm and gregarious New Zealanders. In just a few hours, I noted these differences in our respective vocabularies:

- What we call a *faucet* in America is a *tap* in New Zealand.

- Our everyday custom of eating served up a plateful of differences. On a restaurant menu, the *entree* is the *first course* there, or what we call the *appetizer*. Our restaurant sandwiches carry baffling labels to a New Zealander: such things as reubens, Whoppers, BLTs, and subs. In New Zealand, when ordering soup, there is no distinction between a cup and a bowl. And toast is usually white; if you want whole wheat, you ask for *grown*.

- Finally, as in many countries around the world, when referring to the floors of a building, what Americans call the *first floor* is usually referred to as the *ground floor*. Simple enough, but then outside the United States the next floor is considered the *first floor*, whereas to an American, it would be called the *second floor*.

A glossary of words commonly used in New Zealand that Americans might find different and unusual begins on page 196.

## Pronunciation

Jeff Gibb, a New Zealander and director in the Pacific Asia Travel Association, advises that Americans seem to have difficulty pronouncing place names in New Zealand because they are Maori names. The Maori, of course, are the indigenous people of New Zealand. For example, you'd think the city of Onehunga would be pronounced *One-hunga*, but, in fact, it is *Oh-nay-hung-ar*. Similarly, Petone is not *Pet-one* but *Pet-oh-nay*, and Whakarewarewa is pronounced *Fark-ar-ray-way-ray-wah.* (The Maori are not alone in this regard, as visitors to Wisconsin have learned when they attempt to pronounce two cities there: Oconomowoc and Wauwatosa. Indeed, an entire national TV ad campaign has been based on the pronunciation of Wausau, a city in northern Wisconsin that headquarters the Wausau Insurance Companies.)

Gibb also tells of a New Zealander who wanted to travel from Los Angeles to Oakland, California, but, because of his accent, was repeatedly directed to a flight departing for Auckland.

It has been said that the easy way to learn the special New Zealand accent is merely to pronounce your vowels differently. For example:

The numbers *seven* and *eight* are pronounced *sivin* and *ite*.

One sleeps in a *bade* (instead of *bed*) and at breakfast eats *byecon* and *iggs* (instead of *bacon* and *eggs*).

The statement *Males who have patience use bait to fish on lakes* comes out as *Miles* who have *pyeschence* use *bite* to fish on *likes*.

And *Put the red light on the desk* is said as Put the *rid loit* on the *disk*.

## SOUTH AFRICA

On her first week in the United States, the librarian at the South African Embassy in Washington, D.C., discovered how quickly visitors could trip over commonly used English words. In South Africa (and, indeed, in the United Kingdom as well), mail is referred to as the *post.*

"I went to our embassy reception desk one morning," she relates, "and asked if the post had arrived yet." The attendant nodded, saying, "Oh, yes, ma'am. It arrived at 6:00 A.M." "That early!" she exclaimed, thinking how efficient the U.S. Post Office must be. "Yes. It arrives every morning about that time," the attendant explained. Whereupon he handed her a copy of the *Washington Post* morning newspaper.

As in Australia and New Zealand, South Africans have conceived their own special English dialect. The term *South African English* refers to the English of South Africans, whatever their race, color, or national group. It is described by lexicographers there as truly a "mixed bag." It is not restricted to the language of the "ESSAS" (meaning English-Speaking South Africans), whether white or black, but it is a *lingua franca* for both those to whom English is and many to whom English is not their mother tongue.

So rich is South African English that a 361-page *Dictionary of South African English* was compiled by Dr. Jean Branford and published by Oxford University Press, Cape Town, in 1980. By just paging through this reference book, one can see that South African English is truly a potpourri of words borrowed, loaned, bent, and contrived from three disparate sources: English, Dutch, and native tribal languages.

First, let's clarify the significant presence of Afrikaans, the language of the Afrikaner. Afrikaans is a simplified version of the language of the Netherlands, although the European Dutch view it with a touch of contempt. It is, along with English, one of the two official languages for white South Africans.

One of the most fascinating languages in the world is also found in South Africa. It is Xhosa, which is spoken by the Xhosa people from the region in South Africa known as the Transkei. What makes it so unique is that one of the prominent sounds is a "clicking" sound made far back in the throat, a sound almost impossible to repeat without extensive practice. Anyone who saw the movie *The Gods Must Be Crazy* will probably remember hearing something similar to it, but that was not Xhosa. If you chance upon anyone who speaks it, ask for what will be a memorable demonstration.

Here we will provide a sampling of South African English in order to illustrate that South Africans also have their own special lingo.

The principal city in South Africa is Johannesburg, but to fit quickly into the vernacular you should refer to it as *Joburg*.

Another phrase a visitor to South Africa might encounter is *African time*. It is a jocular reference used by both whites and blacks to being late or unpunctual.

Another colloquialism is to say *to go* when other English-speaking peoples might say *to do*. Thus, when a South African says he or she is going "to go farming" or "go nursing" or "go teaching," it means entering into that full-time activity, rather than merely heading in that direction.

An important homophone (a word with the same sound, but a different spelling and meaning) is the unique South African word *boer*. It is pronounced like the English word *bore* but has several quite different meanings. It can refer to an Afrikaner or to an early Dutch colonist at the Cape, or it can mean a farmer or a fighter in either of the Boer Wars of the late nineteenth century.

There are some things you may want to avoid in South Africa: a *breker* is a "tough or leather-wearing, swaggering motorcyclist type"; a *domkop* is a "fool"; a *krans athlete* is both slang and offensive, as if calling someone a "baboon"; an *outie* is a "down-and-outer," or a "vagrant"; a *ruggerbugger* is slang for a "rather aggressive masculine type who is fanatical about sports and all-male gatherings"; and a *tickey-line* is a "prostitute."

Some possibly confusing words include the following:

A *can* refers to a glass jar, usually two liters in capacity; it is often a container for wine.

*Catfish* along the coast can actually refer to any of several species of octopus.

The *Christmas flower* in South Africa would be the hydrangea, which is always in bloom at Christmas, and not the poinsettia from the Northern Hemisphere.

*The Church* would usually refer to the Anglican Church.

An *eye* also refers to a source or a fountainhead of a spring or river.

A *fuse* is slang for a "cigarette."

A *Harley Davidson* is, especially in the military, a "handlebar mustache."

An *ink pen* is a "fountain pen."

A *kraal* is much the same as an American "corral," but it can also mean a "cluster of huts."

*Meneer* comes from the Dutch and means "Sir" or "Mister."

A *monkey's wedding* refers to simultaneous rain and sunshine, and probably results from the incongruity of such a strange event.

New Year's Eve is often referred to as *Old Year's Night.*

A *painted lady* is a flower, a specie of Gladiolus.

*Paraffin* can either refer to a light rain or be used as slang to denote gin. It also means "kerosene."

A *pirate taxi* is an "unlicensed taxi."

A *school leaving* means "graduation"; in addition, *standard* is used in schools to denote levels, as we use grades in America.

As the Canadians use *eh?* and the French say *n'est-ce pas?* (for, literally, "not so?"), South Africans may be heard to say *is it?* which means "really?" or "Is that so?" Similarly, *isn't it?* is a colloquialism and tag line that invites assent.

The word *kaffir* has no less than six different meanings. It can refer to a member of the Xhosa tribe, or to their language. It is also an abusive term when used in reference to a black person and now, in some parts, is a punishable offense if used. It is also a somewhat obsolete term on the South African Stock Exchange. And it is heard as an element in South African place-names as well as a prefix in the names of flora and fauna of the land.

South Africans might also omit certain words, as in *I'm going on honeymoon* or *He walks to office.* Nouns might be omitted, as in *Come to my twenty-first* (meaning twenty-first birthday) or *She is nursing at the Mental.*

A *springbok* (or springbuck) is not only an antelope or gazelle unique to South Africa, but it is also the following: a national emblem, the traditional name of South African sports teams, soldiers, a channel of commercial radio, and a commonplace name.

This sampler of South African English should implant the fact that, like the other major English-speaking countries, South Africa has adopted hundreds, perhaps thousands, of its own words; and if you're planning an extensive stay there, it would be a good investment to buy the Oxford Press's *Dictionary of South African English.*

## WHERE IS ENGLISH SPOKEN?

Of course, English isn't limited to just the United States, England, Australia, New Zealand, and South Africa. According to a Brigham Young University report, "the sun never sets on English-speaking countries." BYU points to some fifty-five different "brands" of English spoken around the world. The varieties of English spoken among those half-a-hundred countries can produce both comical and serious misunderstandings.

There are three major groupings of English-speaking countries:

1. Countries where English is the native language
2. Countries where English is the official or unofficial language
3. Countries where English is widely studied

What follows is an alphabetical listing of the countries in each of these three categories.

*Countries where English Is the Native Language:*

| | |
|---|---|
| Australia | Barbados |
| Bahamas | Canada (except Quebec) |

Grenada
Guyana
Ireland
Jamaica

New Zealand
Trinidad and Tobago
United Kingdom
United States

*Countries where English Is the Official or Unofficial Language:*

Bahrain
Bangladesh
Botswana
Burma (Myanmar)
Cameroon (west)
Cyprus
Dominican Republic
Egypt
Ethiopia
Fiji
Gambia
Ghana
India
Israel
Kenya
Kuwait
Lesotho
Liberia
Libya
Malawi
Malta
Malaysia

Mauritius
Nauru
Nicaragua
Nigeria
Pakistan
Panama
Papua New Guinea
Philippines
Rhodesia
Senegal
Seychelles
Sierra Leone
Singapore
Somalia
Surinam
Swaziland
Tanzania
Tonga
Uganda
United Arab Emirates
Yemen (southern)
Zambia

*Countries where English Is Widely Studied:*

| | |
|---|---|
| Afghanistan | Ivory Coast |
| Algeria | Japan |
| Angola | Jordan |
| Austria | Libya |
| Brazil | Luxembourg |
| Burkina Faso | Madagascar |
| Burundi | Mexico |
| Central African Republic | Morocco |
| Chad | Nepal |
| China | Netherlands |
| Colombia | Niger |
| Costa Rica | Norway |
| Cuba | Portugal |
| Denmark | Romania |
| Finland | Russia |
| France | Saudi Arabia |
| Gabon | South Korea |
| Germany | Sweden |
| Greece | Switzerland |
| Guinea | Syria |
| Honduras | Thailand |
| Hong Kong | Togo |
| Iceland | Turkey |
| Indonesia | Venezuela |
| Italy | Zaire |

## WHAT YOU NEED TO KNOW ABOUT OTHER
## ENGLISH-SPEAKING NATIONS

- Hong Kong: English English and Chinese (Cantonese) are the official languages. Because it has been a British colony for over a century, the English spoken here is British in both vocabulary and pronunciation.

- Ireland: Both English and Irish Gaelic are official languages. English, with its delightful and distinctive Irish *brogue* is spoken throughout the island, with Gaelic being popular in the west and southwest. A booklet entitled *Irish English/English Irish* provides help in disentangling the delightful Irish gift of gab. It is published by Abson Books, Abson, Wick, Bristol BS15 5TT, England.

- Northern Ireland: The official language is English, but the accent changes noticeably when traveling only a few miles.

- Israel: The official language is Hebrew, with fifteen percent speaking Arabic. English is the language of commerce and, along with French, is spoken by many residents. A booklet entitled *Yiddish English/English Yiddish* provides a glossary of words that pop up in American films, in literature, and on TV; such words as *shlep*, *shlock*, and *shmaltz* are explained. The booklet is published by Abson Books, Abson, Wick, Bristol BS15 5TT, England.

- The Philippines: The official language is Philipino, based primarily on Tagalog, which, to some, may at first sound similar to Spanish. However, there are some eighty different dialects of this language, so English has become the common, unifying language. It is spoken by about forty percent of the population and is especially common in business, education, government, and the tourist trade in the large cities, especially Manila.

- Scotland: English is the common language. Gaelic was the original tongue, and in the north it is currently the second language. Gaelic is also taught in Scottish schools. A booklet entitled *Scottish English/English Scottish* is available in

England from Abson Books, Abson, Wick, Bristol BS15 5TT, England.

- Singapore: In this former British colony, the official languages are Malay, Mandarin, Tamil, and English, with the latter spoken widely in business and government. Mandarin would be the second most popular language.

The so-called English-speaking world is really a mishmash of separate dialects. The lesson is this: The next time you hear English spoken with any kind of British, Australian, or other accent, raise your invisible antenna and listen carefully. The word you hear may not be the word you think it is.

# Part III

# BECOMING A GLOBAL COMMUNICATOR

# 6

# Using Interpreters

*A medium-sized chain of hotels in Florida decided it should try to be more hospitable to its growing number of Japanese visitors. As a first step, it decided to translate certain signs in the hotel, starting with the concierge's desk. A Japanese-born employee was asked for the Japanese word for* concierge, *and it was made into a prominent sign. Several months later, they learned that the actual translation for the Japanese characters supplied to them was the word* pimp.

Regardless of intentions, poor or inadvertent translations can be the curse of clear communications.

For example, the Bible has been translated from its original Aramaic and Greek into Hebrew, Latin, and, finally, English. As a result, scholars through the ages have wrangled over the correct translations of thousands of key, individual words and phrases. For example, in the Old Testament book of Isaiah (7:14), the King James Version (1611) reads:

"Therefore the Lord himself shall give you a sign; Behold, a virgin shall conceive, and bear a son, and call his name Immanuel." In the Revised Standard Version of the Bible (1952), the word virgin is translated and appears as a "young woman." Which interpretation is correct, *virgin* or *young woman*? Could that crucial interpretation have become so imprecise because of the sequence of translations? Or was it due to an individual translator's personal interpretation or preference?

This chapter will not dare to deal with such momentous questions. Instead, mixed in with suggestions on how to work efficiently with an interpreter or translator, we offer examples of muddled, often amusing translations. Incidentally, *translation* usually refers to the *written* form of converting messages from one language to another. *Interpretation* usually refers to the *spoken* form of conversion.

## AVOIDING TRANSLATION SICKNESS

*U.S. News & World Report* magazine has reported that, in Shanghai, tourists were told by their Chinese guide that the population pressure was so great that "the city is pouring out to the skirts." Also, in Tokyo, storefront signs can be seen advertising *Hair Saloon*. And in Argentina, a breakfast menu offered *revolting eggs,* an unintended translation of *huevos revueltos*, which means "scrambled eggs."

Ad Hoc Translations, Inc., a national translation service with offices in New York and Los Angeles, collects similar bloopers. For example, an English rendering of a Chinese poem reads: "He sat under a crying willow." And a medical report stated: "Successful treatment was discontinued on the basis of the patient's death."

---

## Translation Tip

If you want to avoid translation blunders, go to a reputable professional agency for help.

## TRANSLATING THE WRITTEN WORD

Hotel signs around the world seem to be fertile ground for examples of how translations can go awry. Here is a sampling:

In a Paris hotel: Please leave your values at the front desk.

In a Japanese hotel: You are invited to take advantage of the chambermaid.

In a Swiss hotel: Because of the impropriety of entertaining guests of the opposite sex in the bedroom, it is suggested that the lobby be used for this purpose.

In an Acapulco hotel: All of the water in this hotel has been personally passed by the manager.

In a Turkish hotel: Because of a fallibility in our phone system, for room service step outside your door and shout "ROOM SERVICE!"

In a Yugoslavian hotel: The flattening of underwear with pleasure is the job of the chambermaid.

In an Athens hotel: Visitors are expected to complain at the office between the hours of 9 and 11 A.M. daily.

In a Bucharest hotel lobby: The lift is being fixed for the next day. During that time we regret that you will be unbearable.

In a Belgrade hotel elevator: To move the cabin, push button for wishing floor. If the cabin should enter more persons, each one should press a number of wishing floor. Driving is then going alphabetically by national order.

In a Vienna hotel: In case of fire, do your utmost to alarm the hotel porter.

In a Swiss mountain inn: Special today—no ice cream.

In a Japanese hotel (instructions for using the room air conditioner): Cooles and Heates: If you want just condition of warm in your room, please control yourself.

On the door of a Moscow hotel room: If this is your first visit to Russia, you are welcome to it.

## Translation Tip

If you wish to have the written word converted into another language, each word or phrase should not be translated literally. Explain to the translator what message or meaning you wish to convey, and then let the translator decide on the best way to say that in the desired language. For example, one German way to express disbelief is to say, literally, in German, "My hamster is scrubbing the floor." In Thai, to express the maxim *Like father, like son*, one would say, literally, "To know an elephant you must inspect its tail." And in Vietnamese, to convey the idea that when pushed to the limit, a person may react irrationally, one would say, literally, "The crazy dog bites thin hedges."

### COMPUTERIZED TRANSLATIONS

If you have been reading about computerized translation programs eventually solving many of these cross-language obstacles, the key word is *eventually*. At this writing, only a few sophisticated computer programs have been developed to instantly translate spoken language. One of those in Kyoto, Japan—a $128 million computer that took seven years to develop—now understands about fifteen hundred spoken words in Japanese, English, and German. It will take an estimated ten more years before a more practical, affordable system is available to the business world.

At the present time, computerized translations can cause more confusion than clarity. For example, the phrase *Out of sight, out of mind* was entered into one of those computer translation programs and it came out as *invisible thinking*.

Within the next decade, it is predicted that voice recognition will become more common than the keyboard and mouse as a means of communication with your computer. But even that has pitfalls to overcome. The phrase *Give me a new display* can sound like *Give me a nudist play*. And when you mix in a foreign language, with its subtle sounds and intonations, it would seem considerable progress must still be made.

*Computerized translations have not yet been perfected.*

Until the information highway develops this special traffic lane for instant language translations, we will have to deal with people, one-on-one, for translation and interpretation services.

## Translation Tip

Travel stores and catalogs feature handheld electronic translators that are useful for finding single foreign words and maybe even a phrase or two. But since you must punch in each letter of each word, they take time. It is sometimes easier to carry a small foreign language dictionary.

<hr>

## _Translation Tip_

Try to avoid complex quotations, such as from the Bible or Koran, because they are difficult for interpreters to translate quickly and accurately. The same is true, of course, of puns and humor based on wordplay. Also, _consecutive interpretation_ is the term to describe the sequence where one person speaks a few sentences and then pauses to allow the interpreter to translate what was said; this sequence is then repeated until the conversation is over.

<hr>

## PRESIDENTIAL PRATFALLS

U.S. presidents travel with personal interpreters when they visit international capitals and heads-of-state. On one of those occasions, former President Jimmy Carter traveled to Poland and was assigned an interpreter at the last moment. Unfamiliar with Carter's style of speaking, the interpreter made a number of gaffes. Instead of saying Carter "left the United States," the interpreter said Carter had "abandoned the United States." Instead of saying Carter "desired to learn more about life in Poland," the interpreter said Carter "lusted to learn more about life in Poland." And finally, the interpreter committed the biggest goof of all translating Carter's wish to learn more about Poland by saying, in effect, that Carter was "pleased to be here in Poland grasping your secret parts."

When President John F. Kennedy visited West Berlin to express his support, he declared to cheering throngs the famous words "I am a Berliner." As it happened, Kennedy used a local idiom that really said "I am a jelly doughnut."

## TELEPHONE TRANSLATIONS

If you wish to phone overseas and know that you will need translation assistance, this service is now readily available.

---

## *Translation Tip*

When having a transcontinental conversation over the phone, or during videoconferencing, whether speaking through an interpreter or not, there are a few tips to follow. First, speak slowly, clearly, and distinctly. Second, avoid idioms and slang. Third, say numbers slowly, and repeat them. Fourth, at the end of your conversation, summarize key points; then, repeat them in writing and either FAX or send them by mail as back-up confirmation of your discussion.

---

For example, AT&T Language Line® Services is based in Monterey, California, and offers telephone interpretation from English to 140 languages, twenty-four hours a day, seven days a week. No reservations are necessary, and in most cases, an interpreter is available within moments.

Individuals can call a toll free number (1-800-628-8486), and the cost of using an interpreter can be charged on your credit card. Costs include both interpretation services and the long-distance call. Prices vary depending on language and whether the long-distance call is domestic or international. At the time of this writing, prices range from $4.15 to $7.25 a minute.

U.S. companies who need frequent telephone translation services can subscribe under a special onetime fee for account setup and training. For these subscribers, the per-minute cost is significantly reduced.

If calling from abroad, customers can call AT&T's USADirect Service and ask to be connected to Language Line® Services, or they can call (408) 648-5871.

### TIPS FOR TRAVELERS USING INTERPRETERS

As a tourist, you may sign up for a tour led by a local guide whose English is anywhere from passable to excellent. This provides good opportunities to ask about any word usages that interest or puzzle you.

You can also hire a local individual as a guide and interpreter if you wish special care for shopping or sight-seeing. Arrangements can sometimes be made in advance with your local travel agent or through the concierge at your hotel.

If you decide an interpreter is necessary when traveling on business, here are ten tips to consider:

1. Meet with the interpreter in advance. Get acquainted. Explain something about yourself and your business. During this breaking-in period, the interpreter will be listening to your pronunciation, accent, pace, modulation, and word emphasis.

2. Review any technical terminology you may be using. Each business has its own lingo. For example, one executive with a metals company used the word *pickling* to describe a chemical treating process. His interpreter stopped and asked for a few moments to check his dictionary. Finding the definition, he passed it along to the German customer, who responded through the interpreter, "Why does your chemical treating process use cucumbers?"

3. Speak clearly and slowly. Try to construct your messages in groups of short, compact sentences. If the subject is complex, repeat and explain your point in several different ways.

4. Use visual aids wherever possible. Educators advise that we learn more through visual rather than auditory signals.

5. Don't interrupt the interpreter. Interruptions can be disruptive and harmful. Also, don't be concerned if the interpreter seems to spend a longer time repeating your point than you did in presenting it.

6. Don't expect your interpreter to work for over two hours without a rest period. Interpreting is an arduous mental task that requires special concentration and therefore can be very fatiguing.

7. Be courteous and considerate. Make certain your interpreter is treated courteously, is introduced to everyone present, and is allowed time to enjoy a meal.

8. When making a speech to an audience, consider that it will take twice as long to deliver through an interpreter. Consecutive interpretation obviously takes extra time. Practice this with the interpreter before your speech so that you develop a rhythm, and so that you can agree on mutual signals for speeding up, slowing down, or whatever.

9. If confusion arises during your discussions with your business counterpart, ask the interpreter for advice. A good interpreter knows more than just how to translate from one language to another. He or she may detect other problems or misunderstandings from the tone or reaction of the other person.

10. Summarize and confirm all agreements (or disagreements) in writing. Don't rely simply on verbal discussions as a record. Either confirm your discussions in writing before you leave or via FAX or mail when you return home.

## MORE TRANSLATION ANECDOTES

This sign was posted in Germany's Black Forest:

It is strictly forbidden in our black forest camping site that people of different sex, for instance, men and women, live together in one tent unless they are married with each other for that purpose.

**"    "**

From the Soviet Weekly:

There will be a Moscow Exhibition of Arts by 15,000 Soviet painters and sculptors. These were executed over the past two years.

**"  "**

On the menu of a Polish hotel:

Salad a firm's own make; limpid red beet soup with cheesy dumplings in the form of a finger; roasted duck let loose; beef rashers beaten up in the country people's fashion.

**"  "**

From a brochure of a car rental firm in Tokyo:

When passenger of foot have in sight, tootle the horn. Trumpet him melodiously at first, but if he still obstacles your passage then tootle him with vigor.

**"  "**

An American manufacturer of shoes once filmed a tribesman from Kenya for one of its commercials. The man was filmed looking into the camera and saying something in his native language about his hiking shoes. The English subtitle that appeared stated the company's ad slogan, Just Do It. It was later learned that the actual translation was "I don't want these. Give me big shoes."

**"  "**

According to a professor at the University of Sonora in Hermosillo, Mexico, a 1993 Spanish version of the Arizona driver's license manual contained these statements:

Drivers must attend the funeral wakes of children.

Drivers who have donated their eyes, hearts and other organs may ask to have their organs returned to them at any time.

Drivers must ensure that infants are constructed to certain specifications.

**"    "**

A zoo in Budapest warns:

Please do not feed the animals. If you have any suitable food, give it to the guard on duty.

**"    "**

A Swedish furrier advertised:

Fur coats made for ladies from their own skin.

**"    "**

At the United Nations, an interpretation error occurred during a speech by the ambassador from Iraq. He intended to say his nation's enemies were "liars, people of small stature" and hypocrites. The translation came out as "pygmies" which prompted an immediate protest by the ambassador from Zaire.

**"    "**

Finally, the following two signs were observed in a Majorcan shop entrance:

English well speaking

Here speeching American, too

# 7

# Social Conversations around the World

*Stewart Skidmore was visiting Australia for the first time where one evening he found himself invited to a dinner party. He was directed to a seat next to a rather beautiful woman who, according to the host who introduced them, was an accomplished artist. Turning to the woman, Skidmore said, "Oh? Where and when do you display your works?" The woman drew back, shocked, and, for the remainder of the evening, pointedly avoided Skidmore. Later, he learned that in Australia the slang term for a woman's private anatomy was her* works.

Inadvertent language gaffes have probably ruined more budding romances than the combined bad breath of a shipload of romantic sailors.

How does a social conversation begin with American English as the medium of communication? Conversational gambits can produce surprises even in familiar settings. Here's a true story:

A South Carolina businessman entered a cocktail lounge in Rio de Janeiro, Brazil, and took a stool at the bar. Shortly after, an attractive young woman with a short skirt and an abundance of makeup sidled up next to him and issued a friendly "Hello." The man said, "Oh, hello. Do you speak English?" Again, with a warm smile, the girl said "Yes." "How much?" the man asked. Her quick answer: "Fifty dollars."

This chapter will provide tips and advice on acceptable ways to begin conversations with a person—especially one of the opposite sex—in different parts of the world, where both language and cultural differences can present obstacles.

## UNITED KINGDOM

The United Kingdom is considered a land of grace and good manners; for that reason, it serves as a useful "one-size-fits-all"—in other words, what works conversationally in England will probably be good general advice for many countries in the world.

Let's say you are a man and you are in a typical British pub. You wish to start a conversation with an Englishwoman seated nearby. According to British newspaper columnist Jane Gordon, the safest way to start a conversation is to, first, arrange for an introduction. "It's always best to be introduced by some handy, mutual friend," Gordon says.

*Pardon me, but I'm compiling a telephone directory. Can I have your number?*

It would also be impolite to offer to buy a drink or ask for a dance if you have not been introduced. "For *proper* British women [Gordon's emphasis], it is absolutely essential to be introduced by a third party before she can accept a drink or an invitation to dance," Gordon explains.

If an introduction is impossible, the only recourse, according to Gordon, is to be as polite and gracious as possible while saying something like "I hope you don't mind my asking, but . . ."; then posing any one of several standard and innocuous questions, such as:

". . . where are you from in England?"

". . . is this weather typical for the season?"

". . . can you recommend a good restaurant nearby?"

However, a cool reception to any of these sanitized statements is the same message the world over: Quit while you're ahead. If you're lucky, however, an American accent might overcome any slight breach of propriety.

The standard American discussion-starter "What do you do?" (meaning "What do you do as a profession or livelihood?") is considered by some British as too personal, too forward. Among many British, this borders on an invasion of privacy (pronounced *PRIV-ah-cee*, as in the word *privy*). More advice on this from Jane Gordon: "It is becoming more and more accepted in British social circles, especially among the younger crowd, to use that typical Yank question 'What do you do?' but in Britain it's better to work up to that subject rather than introduce it early in the game."

"Safe" subjects for opening conversations are weather, sports, family, and children. The British are also famous for their love of animals, so odds are good that any new acquaintance owns or enjoys pets.

During this breaking-in period, it is important to also know some conversational taboos. It is not indelicate to bring up the subject of royalty and the Royal Family, but *don't criticize*. Your conversational partner might do that, but as Gordon explains, "It's OK for us to do it, but most British don't like to hear it from outsiders."

Other conversational danger areas that usually apply in just about every society are politics, religion, and racial problems. However, once again, if the *other* person introduces these, it is only polite to respond and perhaps engage in light conversation. As Gordon cautions, "You can have intense discussions but they should be friendly and mutually respectful, and don't let humor go out the window."

Another golden rule in England (and elsewhere) would be to avoid risqué jokes, especially in mixed company. They may be shared by groups of the same sex, but it is generally considered inappropriate when both men and women are within earshot.

*Debrett's Etiquette and Modern Manners*, edited by Elsie Burch Donald (Headline Books, London, 1981), is the standard reference book for good manners in Great Britain, equal to our Amy Vanderbilt, Emily Post, and Letitia Baldrige all in one. It offers these additional conversational guidelines:

- When attending a dinner party, no matter how large or small, it is each person's obligation to converse with the people seated on either side.

- Divide the conversation equally between the person on your right and your left side.

- Politics and religion may be discussed, albeit cautiously and carefully monitored by the hostess. A subject that is always taboo is "malicious, ill-natured or ill-worded gossip about someone who is not present."

Here are some tips for socializing with the opposite sex in the United Kingdom:

- Women may offer their hand for a handshake more often than American women.

- Cheek-kissing, however, is done only among old, old friends.

- As for body contact, anything more than a short touch is considered "overstepping the mark," as the British would say. The "Ugly American" is the man who touches excessively or gives a vigorous body hug to a new female acquaintance.

- Among two young people it is acceptable to quickly adopt first names. But in other situations, as a general rule in Great Britain, the safest course is always to use a title (Miss, Mrs., Mr., Doctor, or whatever) until the other person invites you to use his or her first name. This is especially important if there is an age gap where seniority should be respected.

- Speaking of first names, in England, if your name is Dick, it may be better to switch to Richard; also, the name Roger is a slang term from olden days that means "penis"; and a person named Randolph is rarely called Randy, since that word is also used to mean "horny." And there are few, if any, women in England named Fanny, since there that is a crude term for a woman's genitalia.

- Whether you are an American male or female, it's probably wise to avoid excessive or too hurried compliments. Americans are often stereotyped as being forward and boastful, whereas humility, reserve, and a certain self-deprecation are practiced and appreciated in Britain. For example, an American who has won his club championship in tennis might freely volunteer that he "plays a pretty good game of tennis." A Britisher, on the other hand, who competed at Wimbledon would likely merely comment that he or she "played a bit of tennis."

As for the British view of American women, "The main thing British men will notice about American women is how much they talk," writes Jane Walmsley, author of the entertaining book *Brit-Think Ameri-Think*, (Harrap, 1992). American women, on the other hand, are sometimes captivated by merely hearing a British man speak. According to many American women, a British accent seems to serve as almost a verbal aphrodisiac.

And before ending this little conversational tutorial, we should include one shop-worn anecdote about one British word usage that, if you haven't already heard, you probably will soon. One of many versions of this story involves the Englishwoman who enters a car driven by an American man and, as they drive away, remarks, "Oh, I am so glad we have some time to have a bit of intercourse before we arrive at our destination." It is true that in English dictionaries a second, separate definition for *intercourse* is "conversation," but be assured that it is not commonly used by British speakers in this context.

(Note: For additional specific words and phrases that can be booby traps to constructive conversation in Great Britain, see Chapter 4 on the differences between English English and American English.)

## GERMANY

Germany is another country where English is spoken widely, especially in the west-central sector where American and British occupation forces have been stationed for almost fifty years. And this is the first lesson in learning to communicate in Germany: there is distinct regionalism within Germany, with probably the best-known distinction being that the people in the north are more reserved, while the people of the south are more open and expressive.

Here are some generalizations about interpersonal relations in Germany:

- The best conversational openers are the obvious ones: complimentary comments about the country, the city, sports, art, history, music, or whatever.

- Germans are uncomfortable being asked personal questions by people they've just met. Avoid questions about their spouse, family, education, personal finances, or religious affiliations.

- In the eyes of Americans, Germans tend to be straightforward and direct. They seem to say what they think, and they spend little time on small talk. Such matter-of-factness applies whether Germans are complaining or flirting.

- Whispering to another person while in the company of others is not considered rude. On the contrary, it is a display of honest behavior because the topic being discussed does not concern the others who are present.

- The German intonation often makes the language sound aggressive—even angry—but that is usually not the case.

- Few topics of conversation are considered taboo, especially for the postwar generation. Religion and sex are always topics to be treated gingerly, and some Germans may prefer not to talk about the Third Reich and World War II. On the other hand, some may introduce such seemingly sensitive topics as the neo-Nazi movement, Jews in America, and immigration problems in Germany. In that case, the guideline is "If your host brings up the subject, go ahead and respond."

- Some acceptable small talk topics include sports, weather, one's health, pride in the environment, Germany's economic accomplishments since the war, and "safe" items recently in the news.

- American writer Russell Baker claims most Germans lack a sense of humor, but the counterclaim is that they just tend to take life more seriously than others. Visit any *gasthaus* (beer garden) in Bavaria, especially during Octoberfest, and merriment abounds.


Other courtesies to note are these:

- When introduced, German women will usually proffer their hand for a handshake.

- Always use titles (*Frau* means "Mrs.," *Fraulein* means "Miss," and *Herr* means "Mr.") when first introduced. Don't immediately jump to first names; continue using titles until you are invited to use first names.

- When answering the phone, Germans usually begin by stating their names, or they say *Bitte* which, roughly, means "Please."

## ITALY

Professor of Italian Studies Hugh Shankland writes: "Spontaneous courtesy and agreeable informality characterize most Italians' direct dealings with outsiders. The popular image of Italian men as slavish attenders on women is quite fallacious. There is little pointless gallantry: men do not feel obliged to open and shut doors for women getting in and out of cars for instance."

English-speaking visitors are particularly lucky because English is so popular in Italy. One reason is that Italian youths follow British and American movies, pop music, and videos.

While popular American English words and terms, even slang and advertising slogans, will pop up in daily conversation, this does not mean Italians are fluent. But their special interest in English does allow for quick start-up conversations.

Also, it pays to try to learn a bit of Italian. It is an especially lovely language, not too difficult to learn, and most Italians will be appreciative and overlook your mistakes. Opening topics for conversation are plentiful in Italy, for example, food, wine, history, art, fiestas, the weather, the cinema, opera, fashion, and soccer.

Single American women traveling in Italy should be prepared for plenty of attention. In fact, *hunted* is one word that pops up in some guidebooks. The best way to deal with this is to, first, ignore it; second, to make your messages of rejection clear in both vocal and body languages; and, third, to drop all your reserve and "have a good shout," as Shankland advises. Further, Shankland points out that even Dante spoke of the appropriateness of treating rudeness with rudeness in return.

Shaking hands at the beginning and ending of a social contact is quite common in Italy. Close friends and relatives may kiss cheeks (go to your left, their right, first). Good male friends will embrace. And you may see good men friends strolling arm-in-arm on Italian streets.

Respect titles preceding a person's name: doctor, professor, engineer, etc.

Italians are very expressive with the hands and face. Italy is considered the "Garden of Eden" when it comes to creating and using gestures.

## FRANCE

For an American attempting to communicate in France, it is important to recognize a dichotomy that exists there. First, the French are immensely proud of their language. In fact, many resent the intrusion of popular English words that may infest their daily lives. This pride is especially strong in Paris and its environs and therefore makes it difficult to communicate. Many Americans, trying their amateurish college French, are often met with apparent coolness. On the other hand, a warmer reception comes from two groups: the people throughout the rest of France, and young people. With each of these groups, an American with a dictionary in hand and a smile on the face will find the conversational road less bumpy.

Next, it is important to remember that *etiquette* is a French word. Demonstrations of grace, politeness, and proper behavior at all times will increase respect and thus improve the chances of affable conversation.

As for conversational subjects, there is a wide range to choose from. The French are proud of their educational system, their literary heritage, their artistic accomplishments, and their world-renowned cuisine. Furthermore, once the first conversational barricades are breached, the French love engaging in spirited debate, especially if logic is the fulcrum. As for taboos, one gaffe is to lump the French with the Belgians.

Appealing topics for conversation include jazz, the cinema, history, cycling, wines, and sports.

## RUSSIA

English is taught extensively throughout Russia. In fact, it is said that there are more teachers of English in Russia than there are people in the United States who speak Russian. Therefore, in Russia, it is often fairly easy to strike up a conversation with someone, albeit not in fluent English.

A Russian, when introducing himself or herself, will probably utter *three* names: first comes the Christian, or given, name (in America, we simply say "the first name"); then comes the father's Christian name; and, finally, the surname. These treble names also come in masculine form or feminine form. Therefore, a man might be called *Ivan* (his Christian name), *Petrovich* (taken from his father's Christian name, *Peter*), *Suslov*. But a woman would feminize those in this fashion: *Natasha Petrovna Suslova*. When you do not know a Russian very well, you should address him or her by using the first two names.

Also, don't be surprised if couples have different surnames. Women in Russia do not automatically take their husband's name and often retain their own.

Men and women, when greeting one another, will very likely shake hands—Russians usually shake hands each and every time they meet an acquaintance. Cheek-kissing (three times, alternating cheeks) is done only by good friends, and it is done both man-to-man and woman-to-woman.

Friendships are expressed openly. Not only will good women friends walk arm-in-arm or hand-in-hand, but good men friends will do the same. It is not uncommon to see two Russian men walking in public arm-in-arm or hand-in-hand; this merely signifies good friendship and does not necessarily carry any sexual connotation or relationship.

As for conversational topics, few families in Russia were left untouched by World War II, and the subject is taught extensively in Russian schools. Therefore, most Russians are prepared to discuss at least some aspect of that enormous conflict.

Since the late 1980s and Gorbachev's *perestroika* and *glasnost*, most Russians are perfectly ready to talk about life and daily conditions. In fact, just obtaining the necessities of life is one of the chief concerns—and topics of conversation—in Russia today.

Criticism of the government is also unfettered, and both television and the press now offer a menu of both commentary and controversy.

Another likely question aimed at you will be "What is life really like in the United States?" Most Russians are genuinely interested. So be prepared for both penetrating questions as well as queries that suggest a distorted view of American life, such as "Does everyone in the United States carry a gun?"

When visiting private homes, or at official dinners, the exchange of toasts and short speeches are very common. Each course is washed down with vodka, toasts, and more vodka. Groups usually remain seated around the dinner table and continue talking into the late hours of the evening.

## JAPAN

Advising on male/female conversations in Japan becomes relatively easy. The reason is that they are unlikely to occur except in staged business entertainment situations. Casual, social conversations between the sexes are rare, as is being invited into a Japanese home to meet the family.

Another impediment is the language itself. Even though learning English is becoming a national passion in Japan, channels of communication are still cluttered and sticky.

For Americans, unless one spends years and years studying the language, it is very difficult to communicate comfortably with the Japanese. Masako Watanabe, an exchange student in journalism at the University of Wisconsin, tells how an American student walked up to her and tried to say in Japanese "You're cute" (*kawaii* in Japanese). Instead, he mistakenly used *kowai* which stated "You're scary."

Another difficulty comes in the way Americans and Japanese use yes and no. First, the Japanese have great difficulty saying no to anything because it is ingrained that anything negative disrupts the harmony of a situation. Consequently, they seem to say yes to almost anything—which should be interpreted as "Yes, I hear what you're saying . . . but that doesn't necessarily mean I agree with you."

Watanabe also points out that the Japanese would respond to a negatively stated question (for example, "Don't you have a car?") differently than would Americans. To answer that question, the Japanese would say, "Yes"—meaning "Yes, I do not have a car."

Not only is the language complex, but there is also so much *unsaid* among the Japanese. Edward T. Hall, the famed anthropologist, explains that the Japanese communicate as twin siblings would, with much intuitive understanding.

On the Japanese side, American idioms and slang make our language a briar patch of frustration for them. This leaves little room for easy, casual male/female conversation. Still, here are some customs that both sexes should bear in mind when West meets East:

- Bowing is the traditional greeting, and it is not (as many Americans believe) an act of subservience. It is a sign of humility and respect in a land where both those qualities are highly prized.

- Proper posture is also regarded as important, so avoid slouching in your chair or plunking your feet up on the nearest cocktail table.

- Never, never, never do anything that will bring any form of embarrassment to a Japanese man or woman. This causes the famous *loss of face*, the kiss of death for any relationship throughout all the Orient.

- Never express affection in public, except with children.

- Smiling may be a way of hiding embarrassment. Similarly, showing the wide-open mouth (as when laughing uproariously) is considered rude. ⚘

- Body language to know: Pointing with your fingers and loud sniffling of the nose should be avoided; direct eye contact is not common; and handshakes may be given with a limp hand.

- Western women may be treated with either indifference or with abject curiosity. This is no reflection on you or your gender. It is a result of centuries of Japan being such a male-oriented society.

- When American businessmen are entertained in Japan, it usually comes in the form of going to a nightclub. Female hostesses will lavish attention, and the ones that speak the best English will probably be assigned to American guests. There will be much attentiveness, giggling, and serving of food and drinks. It is important to realize this flirtatious behavior is purely a custom and not due to one's magnetic charms.

- Finally, any conversation in Japan is likely to be roundabout, punctuated with periods of silence, excessively polite, and devoid of strong declarations or opinions.

## THAILAND

British diplomat Derek Tonkin writes that "Thais have no chips on their shoulders. Visitors are welcomed as equals. Racial and religious prejudice is virtually unknown. Buddhist tolerance goes hand in hand with intense national pride."

Yet there are two sacrosanct rules of conversational behavior while in Thailand. First, show respect for the Thai monarchy; second, show equal respect and sensibility toward the Buddhist religion.

Thais also respect the elderly, a sense for the supernatural, and both good and bad omens.

Most Westerners find the Thais very sociable. Even the Thai greeting—the *wai*—is unique and graceful: the Thais press their palms together in front of their chest, in a prayerlike gesture. This greeting has many nuances—who *wais* whom, how high the hands are held, and so on—so don't *wai* indiscriminately. The best, basic response is a smile and nod of the head.

In fact, a smile is essential body language for anyone visiting Thailand. Thais smile when they are happy or when they are embarrassed. For example, a motorist who splashes water on you will apologize by smiling because it's his or her way of saying sorry.

Further, when a pretty Thai woman smiles, it is not a "come hither" gesture. As Tonkin advises, "Many Thai women smile most of the time. It is simply their way of looking prettier."

All this nonverbal language is important to understand in Thailand because the Thai language is so exotic for Westerners. Written Thai is one continuous stream, without spaces between words and with little capitalization or punctuation. It is also a *tonal language* in that the same word means different things depending on whether the tone is high or low, rising or falling.

Therefore, when visiting Thailand, learn about body language. For example, it is important to know the following: Never pat someone on the top of the head, because that is where one's spirit resides; and never point the sole of the shoe toward another person, because that is considered an insult.

Westerners—both male and female—will have little trouble finding entertainment and socialization in Thailand, all for a price, of course. Bangkok is alive with nightlife—discos, go-go bars, nightclubs, massage parlors—take your choice. Western women visitors are welcomed, but it is best to travel in pairs or in the company of men. Just be prepared for some possible eye-opening scenes and floor shows in certain bars and clubs.

In summary, grace and friendliness characterize the Thai people, and you will find few obstacles to conversation.

## KOREA

South Koreans have been called "the Irish of the Orient." This is because they can be likeable, affectionate, passionate people who enjoy partying and imbibing.

Yet there is another side that prevents them from showing emotion or sentiment. For example, although South Koreans are always polite and courteous, it is sometimes difficult for them to express those feelings.

As with other Oriental countries, understanding and speaking the language is usually out of reach for most temporary Western visitors. For that reason it is important to understand Korean *behavior* for a visitor to communicate in this interesting land.

Here are some general customs worth noting:

- Seniority and age are highly respected. This ranges from rising on a bus and offering your seat to an elderly person to showing special respect for the most senior businessperson at a meeting.

- Married women in Korea who adhere to traditional ways will wear their hair in a neat, round bun, while unmarried women favor a pigtail.

- On the other hand, more modern Korean women will smoke, drink, petition for divorce, and vigorously support the feminist movement.

- In spite of this, the male rules in Korean society, and women are usually subordinated.

- As a result of this duality, Korean women will be flattered if a Western visitor opens a door for them or practices "ladies first."

- Direct eye contact is not practiced as much in Korea as in the United States. In fact, direct eye contact is considered impolite. Also, a handshake may be weak rather than firm, and all other body contact is avoided.

- Avoid first-name usage until invited to do so.

- Blowing your nose in public is considered gauche, but belching is not.

- As in Japan and other parts of the Orient, *face* is all important, so avoid any action or statement that could bring embarrassment.

- Heavy drinking and even drunkenness are not frowned upon in Korea. In fact, as in Japan, this is considered a typical way to become friends.

- Social entertainment often involves *karaoke* singing. And even if your musical repertoire is limited to "Happy Birthday," stand up and sing it! Message: the shrinking violet will never survive in Korea.

- When invited to a home, your hostess may be too busy to eat with guests. Showing genuine affection and warmth to children is especially endearing to Korean parents.

- People, especially women, will cover their mouths when laughing.

When it comes to attitudes of man-meets-woman, Koreans and many other Orientals view such social intercourse as normal and expected. Western attitudes are regarded as reserved, puritanical, and curiously restrictive. As a result, men in these societies definitely have an easier time taking initiatives in the man/woman relationship. Conversely, an aggressive, bold Western woman will find difficult sledding in these countries.

An American businesswoman tells of one trip she made to South Korea where a Korean businessman said to her, "I am sorry about your husband." Not comprehending, she asked what he meant. "Oh," he said, "I noticed your wedding ring and so I assumed you are a widow." "Why would you conclude that?" she asked politely. His answer was "Because if he were still alive, I assume you would still be at home taking care of your home and family."

## CHINA

Confucius, who was born 551 years before Christ, wrote the first book on proper behavior . . . strong evidence that good etiquette and behavior are important among the Chinese.

When considering customs and behavior among the Chinese today, there are three distinct groupings or regions of people: (1) the one billion people in the vast region we call Mainland China, (2) the island of Taiwan, with its political separateness from the Communist China, and with its strong business ties to the United States, and (3) the colony of Hong Kong, one of the most exotic, eclectic, and vibrant cities in the world.

## *Hong Kong*

Let's start with Hong Kong. It has been a British colony since the mid-eighteenth century; consequently, English is widely spoken there. And, because it is one of the busiest natural ports in the world, travelers have enjoyed the social life of Hong Kong for centuries. Accordingly, it is not difficult for men and women to . . . let's use the word *socialize* while in Hong Kong.

Because Hong Kong is a center of world commerce, the inhabitants are accustomed to meeting and dealing with people of every nationality. Little will surprise them. Nonetheless, the wise visitor will do some homework and consider the following traits of the Chinese culture:

- Never embarrass someone, purposely or inadvertently. Such *loss of face* is the worst possible social offense.

- Respect their religions (Buddhism, Taoism, Confucianism, and Christianity). Also, respect their reverence for ancestors and the elderly, their beliefs in what we would call *superstitions*, and their devotion to family.

- The handshake has become the most common form of greeting among both men and women. However, among the older generation and traditionalists, you might observe the following greeting: the right hand is made into a fist and then covered with the left hand, held at chest height, and accompanied by a small bowing motion with the head.

- Modesty and humility are prized. Compliments are often deflected because it would be poor manners to agree.

- In the higher circles of business and among the well-heeled strata of society in Hong Kong, British decorum often prevails: formal dinners, cocktail parties, afternoon teas, fashion shows, visiting the race track, and so on.

- For the man who seeks "pleasuring," as one veteran observer calls it, there is a large arena of possibilities. The best example is found in the hundreds of "hostess clubs" teeming with *cheong-sam* clad women selected for their beauty, charm, and intelligence. Consequently, within these clubs, man/woman talk is a given. For a tightly monitored fee, conversation is readily available to anyone who enters; and for higher fees, more than just talk is readily available.

- What does an American businesswoman do when socializing in Hong Kong? One woman told me when she accompanied her husband, who was also her business partner, she "just removed my wedding ring and pretended we were on a date." She explained, "That put the others, who were our business contacts, at ease."

### Taiwan

Turning to Taiwan, visitors will notice many similarities with Hong Kong: English is freely spoken, the nightlife is equally abundant, respect for the Chinese culture is welcomed and appreciated, and, with commerce being the overarching priority, the Taiwanese also are accustomed to receiving and accepting people from many other cultures. What distinguishes Taiwan from Hong Kong is the British influence that is so prevalent in Hong Kong.

Taiwan (officially, the Republic of China) was created in 1949 when refugees fled the Communist onslaught on the mainland. As a result, there is a long-standing antipathy among the Taiwanese for the government of the Mainland. That has eased somewhat in recent years, however, and there are even signs of cautious reconciliation.

For the American businessperson visiting Taiwan, the atmosphere will be businesslike, festive, and generally comfortable. Women play an active role in all aspects of business, and Americans of both sexes are welcomed because the United States is Taiwan's largest customer.

As for tips on general behavior, just remember that the Chinese culture prevails: etiquette, grace, and patience are valuable traits. Respect, humility, politeness, and reverence for the elderly and for other traditions are also important. Further, the Taiwanese are proud of their special heritage and history, and particularly of the artistic treasures they "rescued" from the Communist armies as they swept southward in 1949.

## *Mainland China*

Let's turn now to the colossus of Mainland China, or, more properly, The People's Republic of China (PRC).

Visitors should bear in mind that the people of the PRC are now emerging from a thirty-year period (1949–1979) of strict, conservative social management. During that period, social relationships between men and women were so subordinated that, according to writer Boye DeMente, when young parents were asked by their children about the differences between men and women, the reply was, "Men smoke and women don't."

Today, in the workplace, many women can be seen holding equally responsible positions with men, but sexual relations among Chinese couples is still a sensitive subject. Further, fraternization between Chinese and foreigners is regarded as a serious offense.

Whether in business or as a tourist, communication is not an easy matter for an American in the PRC. Here are some tips to bear in mind:

- The telecommunications system has made great strides since the 1980s, but conducting routine business and other forms of telephonic communication is still difficult.

- Communication by letter or FAX is also encumbered by the need for translation into Chinese.

- One basic bit of knowledge concerns the names of individuals. Mr. Hua Quo is referred to as "Mr. Hua" because that is his family name; the other name is his given name.

- The Chinese may ask rather direct, personal questions— such as why you are not married, or how much money you make each year. Don't take offense; this is just natural curiosity.

- Like the Japanese, periods of silence may occasionally occur during business meetings or social conversations. This has no special meaning other than a pause in the discourse. Don't feel obliged to step in and fill the void.

- Avoid forcing the Chinese into a verbal corner where they must say no. This is difficult for them. To avoid a direct negation, the Chinese may say "it is inconvenient" or "that is very difficult."

- In public settings, such as in retail stores and on public transportation, be prepared to be pushed and shoved a bit. The Chinese do not automatically form queues, or lines.

- Also, at the dinner table, be prepared for the *sounds* of eating—slurping, sipping, belching. This is not considered rude. Also, spitting in public is accepted because it is regarded as ridding the body of a waste.

- Also, as a foreigner, be prepared for stares. In some parts of China, a foreigner is such a rarity that the locals will stare long and openly. And if you have red or blond hair, are exceptionally tall, or stand out in any manner, you might even have small crowds assemble to look at you.

- When meeting a large group of people (such as a classroom of children) be prepared for applause. Groups of Chinese often greet and bid good-bye to guests with such hand-clapping.

In summary, before my first trip to China, a veteran of that country offered me this general advice: "When in China, speak and act as though your elderly and wealthy aunt has just asked you how much you think she should leave you in her will."

For an excellent reference book on behavior among the Chinese, turn to Boye DeMente's *Chinese Etiquette and Ethics in Business* (NTC Business Books, Lincolnwood, IL, 1989).


## GENERAL COMMENTS ON THE *S* WORD—SEX

Sex-for-pay is available around the world in both expected and unexpected locales. For starters, prostitution is legal in countries like

Denmark, Holland, and Thailand, albeit confined to particular zones or streets. (As for those unexpected spots, a few years ago, the citizens of Milwaukee, Wisconsin, with its conservative German-Polish heritage, were shocked when newspapers revealed a local "escort service" that had on its customer list the names and phone numbers of over 600 local men.)

Whatever the extent of "boy-meets-girl" for the S word, when traveling the world as tourist, student, or businessperson, it is a terribly risky pastime. While disease is currently the greatest concern, the possibilities of theft, injury, and worse are also prevalent.

On my first visit to Amsterdam, I was taken to the famous red zone, where ladies of the night display themselves in large picture windows. When I asked, "Is it dangerous to be in this area?" my Dutch business host and guide replied, "No, no, no. Although they did find a trunk recently containing a dismembered male. They have ruled out suicide."

Female visitors are, of course, counseled to avoid these and other dangerous zones. Your hotel concierge can advise which areas to avoid.

Tour guides in Manila boast that they have the most "accommodating" red light zone of all. "First come the restaurants, where you can obtain a good meal," they explain. "Then, right next door are the discos, where you can obtain companionship. Next are the hotels, where you can obtain a room. And, conveniently next to the hotels are the medical clinics, where you can obtain any necessary medications. Finally, last in row are the churches, where you can hope to obtain forgiveness."

The moral issue aside, a chief concern of Americans traveling abroad who seek man/woman "conversation" should be *safety*. Safety involves avoiding not only disease, but also theft, blackmail, and worse.

This closing anecdote helps epitomize how American English can be confounding in social situations and especially when it comes to man/woman talk:

> George Poppas is Greek-born and now a prominent businessman in Wisconsin. He first came to America as a teenager and distinctly remembers hearing his high school

friends talk about dating, parking on lover's lane, and necking. "I knew about kissing and touching and slow dancing," Poppas recalls, "but I couldn't possibly imagine what was arousing about two people rubbing necks together. In fact, I tried rubbing my neck with my hands and it didn't do a thing for me."

# 8

# The Tower of Business Babel

*One bright Sunday morning, sitting with my German manager in the manicured garden of his home in Baden-Baden, we were discussing ideas for next year's marketing plan. Midway in our conversation my German host, Willi S., turned abruptly toward me and said, "Here. Let me pull some worms from your nose." My gasp caused Willi to bolt straight up and ask, "What's wrong?" "What did you say about* worms?" *I asked. Confused, Willi replied, "I said 'Let me pull some worms from your nose.'" And then, rather defiantly, he added, "What's wrong with that? You say that in English too." After some head-scratching and further probing, we discovered what Willi was referring to was the American phrase* Let me pick your brain.

For Americans, *picking worms from someone's nose* sounds positively repulsive. Yet, ironically, why our phrase *picking one's brain* is benign and perfectly acceptable is beyond reason.

To further confuse matters, as Willi and I dissected the two idioms, we discovered the German phrase about picking worms was more akin to the English metaphor *harder than picking hen's teeth.* What had happened was that, understandably, in the English section of Willi's brain, the three separate phrases had become comingled and confused.

It happens easily enough, but it clearly demonstrates how one innocent phrase on a bright Sunday morning can throw a *spanner* (British for "monkey wrench") into any business discussion.

Several years ago, I helped conduct a survey of over two hundred American international business travelers to learn how business discussions sometime become derailed by misunderstandings of seemingly common words and phrases. Significantly, 61 percent of those executives replied that they always conduct business in English, while the remainder did so part of the time. None replied that

*Asking the whereabouts of the "restroom" could create confusion.*

business was conducted totally in a foreign language. And, further-more, 80 percent reported that it was difficult to communicate with their international counterparts because of the latter's incomplete understanding of American English.


## FROM BOARDROOMS TO BATHROOMS

American lingo can pop up in the unlikeliest places. Let's start not in the business boardroom, but instead in the equally ubiquitous office bathroom.

Have you ever considered the multiple euphemisms we Americans use just to designate the toilet? Here is a partial list:

| | |
|---|---|
| washroom | bathroom |
| potty | men's room/ladies' room |
| sandbox | boys' room/girls' room |
| restroom | WC (British for "water closet") |
| throne | commode |
| the conveniences | the facilities |
| gentlemen/ladies | lads/lassies |
| knights/ladies | guys/dolls |
| cowboys/cowgirls | the used beer department |
| the altar | biffy |
| cloakroom | indoor plumbing |
| the john | the can |
| the gents | lavatory |
| the head (U.S. Navy and Marines) | the latrine (U.S. Army) |
| powder room | the outhouse |

Can you add others? And, when we wish to *use* the bathroom, we have a separate collection of masked words and phrases:

wash my hands

visit the restroom

take a tinkle

use the facilities

have a wash (British)

spend a penny (British)

use the plumbing

make a pit stop

hit the head

powder my nose

make a call of nature

take a pee

stop my back teeth from floating

go Number One / Number Two

go wee wee

How does this list of doublespeak affect the conduct of business?

A Houston businessman tells of one occasion when he and an American associate were visiting oil-drilling customers in Saudi Arabia. The Houstonian's associate was experiencing digestive problems and, during the meetings and later at dinner, frequently excused himself, asking, "Where is the little boy's room?" Toward the end of the evening, during one of these absences, the Saudi host turned to the Houstonian and gently inquired, "Am I to take it that your friend likes little boys?"

The moral here is: Whenever visiting another country, it is always useful to learn the word for "toilet" in the local language. Yet, even that is not always guaranteed. Read what happened to an American aerospace industry executive, fluent in several Oriental languages, during a trip to the Orient:

The executive had spent four days in Taiwan speaking Chinese and then traveled to South Korea, which, of course, required an abrupt switch to Korean. On his arrival, needing to visit the bathroom, he tried to remember the correct words for "men's room" in Korean. When he uttered what he thought were the correct words, he was greeted with dead silence. Fortunately, someone who knew English began to laugh—as did the others when he explained what the American had asked for was not the men's room but, instead, a whorehouse.

## WORKADAY WORDS OR BUSINESS BOMBSHELLS?

Here are two relatively common words—*parallel* and *scratch*—that demonstrate how our language can sometimes be a veritable minefield.

An American businessman from the Midwest concluded his discussions with his Japanese customer with "Well, our thinking is in parallel." They bid good-bye, but weeks and then months passed with no further word from the customer. Finally, frustrated, the American phoned and inquired what had happened. "Well," the Japanese replied, "you used a word I didn't understand. *Parallel.* I looked it up in my dictionary and it said *parallel* means 'two lines that never touch.'" The Japanese had concluded that the American thought their thinking was *apart.*

The word *scratch* means "to scrape mildly, as with the fingers, to relieve itching or irritation of the skin." But such irritation is nothing compared to the confusion *scratch* can cause when used in other contexts. Here are three examples:

After a two-week, total immersion course in Japanese, an employee of an Asia-Pacific sales operation tried to order lunch by himself using his new language. Unknowingly, he asked the waitress for both french fries and regular potatoes. When so informed by a colleague, he turned to the Japanese waitress and said, "Scratch the potatoes." The result: total incomprehension.

A facsimile message was sent from a U.S. manufacturer concerning certain parts "made from scratch." The reply from the overseas customer clearly indicated that phrase was misunderstood. The customer replied, "Think the word *scratch* should be *sketch*."

An American businessman, addressing a Chinese audience, mentioned in his opening remarks that he was " . . . tickled to death to be in China." After his interpreter converted those words, there was a murmur from the audience. It seems his interpreter had explained, "The American gentleman says he scratched himself until he died in order to be here."

Here are a couple of other examples of business bombshells:

Allen Fredericks, associate editor of *Travel* magazine tells of a group of Chinese visitors who once asked him, "Please, sir, what is a *turkey?*" Knowing that our traditional Thanksgiving fare was largely unknown in China, Fredericks went to great lengths to explain about the Pilgrims, the wild turkey, and how it was identified with Thanksgiving. "Well, then, sir," the questioner persisted, "what does it mean when an American says, 'Let's get this turkey on the road'?"

Another American business group visiting China was described as having representatives from "blue-chip" companies, only to have their host quickly ask what *blue chip* meant. When it was explained about the different colored chips used in poker and other games of chance, the

Chinese host aloofly sniffed at them, "They are not welcome. We do not condone gambling in China."

Now that you've seen how American "corporatese" can sound like gibberish to other ears, perhaps you'll look on the following list of common business terms with greater sensitivity:

| American Business Term | What's That? |
| --- | --- |
| direct mail | Is there *in*direct mail? |
| legal eagle | What's an *il*legal eagle? |
| downtime | Is there *up* time? |
| Will it float? | Why is that important? |
| shotgun approach | Shotguns hurt people. |
| the bottom line | bottom of what? |
| red ink, black ink | We favor blue ink. |
| pigeonholed | Are pigeonholes different? |
| dog and pony show | Just slides will do. |
| a catch-22 situation | What happened to catch-21? |

## BUSINESS ABBREVIATIONS AND ACRONYMS

A business riddle: What is one of the most commonly used words in business today that is (1) used as both a noun and a verb, (2) an abbreviation for a longer word, and (3) derived from the *sound* of the word's first syllable but not the actual spelling of the word? The answer, of course, is *FAX*. (Incidentally, Thomas Fuller, a seventeenth-century theologian, would be thrilled. According to the *New York Times*, it was he who first used the word *facsimile*, which he took from the Latin, *fac simile*, meaning "make similar.")

Americans seem to have a love affair with such abbreviations and acronyms. Three examples of long-lived abbreviations and acronyms in American business are SOP (standard operating procedure), ASAP (as soon as possible), and SNAFU (situation normal—all fouled up), all of which probably go back over forty years to WW II. (Oops! See how they just pop up everywhere?)

They have been joined in recent years by IRA (which has absolutely nothing to do with the Irish Republican Army), ESOP (pronounced *EE-sop*, for employee stock option plan), MBO (management buyout), and LBO (for leveraged buyout—*leverage* being just another obscure American way of saying "We went out and borrowed a whole pile of money to do this.")

P&Ls (for profit-and-loss statements) have become a staple in the business lexicon, but, oddly, no such abbreviation has been adopted for the P&L's sibling, the corporate balance sheet. Similarly, office desks are now sprinkled with PCs, and offices are quickly installing *e-mail*, meaning an electronic mail system (nee answering machine). Xerox has become synonymous with photocopying, much to the chagrin of the trademark protectors at the Xerox Corporation.

As for government-originated abbreviations that have invaded the business world, space will not permit the cataloging of all of them. That's probably worthy of an entirely separate gazette. Just to make the point, however, here are a few. See how many you can identify:

| | | |
|------|------|--------|
| IRS | AG | CIA |
| HUD | HEW | DEA |
| DOD | OPIC | INS |
| GAO | OPEC | UNESCO |
| FED | UN | FAA |
| OSHA | STR | FTC |
| SEC | FBI | ICC |

And the lists go on:

- American offices are populated with CEOs, MBAs, CFOs, PR'ers, COOs, CPAs, Ph.D.'s, VPs, and, of course, SR. VPs. We have Dir. (for director), and Mgr. (for manager), and Asst. and Assoc. for their underlings.

- Payments and shipping departments use such abbreviations as CIA (cash in advance), FOB (free on board), COD (cash on delivery), C&F (customs and freight), FAS (free alongside ship), DEC (declaration of export certificate), and LC (letter of credit).

- The personnel department is now referred to as HR (for human resources), and they are mired in COLAs (cost-of-living adjustments), SOPs (stock option plans), perks, NMI (no middle initial), and 401 (C) savings plans.

- Accountants live or die by D&B (Dun & Bradstreet) credit reports; GAAP (generally accepted accounting principles); FASB (Financial Accounting Standards Board, pronounced *Faz-bee*) rulings; P/E (price/earnings) ratios; ROI (return-on-investment); ROA (return-on-assets); FIFOs and LIFOs (dealing with inventories); and one fictional inventory system waggishly called FISH (for first in, still here).

- A critical part of any company is R&D (research and development), to whom the QC (quality control) and QA (quality assurance) people are often attached. And let's not forget all those MIS (management information systems) people who operate and massage all those computers.

Finally, PR people can be found in almost every type of American business. That, of course, stands for "public relations," populated by people who are supposed to be experts in communications. Yet, experts though they may be, the PR profession itself has not yet found a standard label for its craft. In some companies, the PR function operates under the label of corporate affairs, corporate communications, or community affairs. Outside the United States, the term *public relations* is not well known and does not translate well into, say, either French or Spanish. There, if the function does exist, it is probably referred to as "social responsibilities." A related area of confusion arises with the word *publicity*, which in places like Britain, France, and the Latin world is used to mean *advertising* and not free, editorial articles or stories.

Once again, put yourself in the place of a foreigner trying to comprehend American business language and, instead, being confronted with abbreviations seemingly thrown out at random, as if on a pair of dice. As the King of Siam might say to Anna in *The King And I*, it . . . "is a puzzlement."

## SHOCKING SIMILES

Next to our addiction for abbreviations and acronyms comes our soft spot for similes, those colorful figures of speech that compare two essentially unlike things usually using the connecting word *as* or *like*. For example:

> A Chicago businessman, hosting a visitor from Hong Kong, glanced out of his office window and announced, "Wow! It's raining like cats and dogs outside!" The Chinese jumped up and ran to the window, anxious to witness this astounding phenomenon, perhaps because in Hong Kong cooked dog is considered a delicacy.

Here's a suggestion. During your daily business discussions, discreetly start accumulating your own list of strange similes that might make conversations with a foreigner "clear as mud."

Here are more examples to help attune your ear:

fast as quicksilver

quick as a cat

crazy like a fox

flatter than a pancake

dead as a doornail

blind as a bat

alike as two peas in a pod

cool as a cucumber

angry as an open wound

right as rain

honest as the day is long

happy as a lark

bad as sin

bald as a billiard ball

like a wolf in sheep's clothing

cautious as a cat in a room full of rockers

cheap as dirt

soft as a baby's bottom

cold as a witch's tit

sweet as a mother's milk

slick as snot

busy as a bee

## BUMBLED BRAND NAMES

Every student of International Marketing 101 has learned the story of how the Chevrolet division of General Motors named one of its models the Nova, only to later learn that in Spanish the words *no va* mean "it doesn't go." And in Belgium, GM's tag line Body by Fisher was translated into Flemish as "Corpse by Fisher."

Another old standard tells how Pepsi's Come Alive slogan came out of the translation process in Taiwan as "Pepsi brings your ancestors back from the grave."

Lesser known, perhaps, are these:

A telephone system known as the Chat Box became, in French, the *Cat Box*. (*Chat* is the French word for "cat.")

A brand of beer in Australia known as Four X could not be marketed in the United States because a line of condoms called Fourex had already been established here.

Parker Pen's well-known Jotter ballpoint pen could not be marketed with that name in some Latin countries because that word also happened to be the slang for *jockstrap*.

The Dutch are known for their impish sense of humor, so it shouldn't have surprised me when my business guest from Amsterdam once asked me, "I know what Preparation H is, but tell me, what ever happened to Preparations A through G?"

If you, as a businessperson, would be embarrassed by making any of these inadvertencies that would be understandable. Now consider for a moment that even the very word *embarrassment* has caused embarrassment.

> Several decades ago, The Parker Pen Company marketed bottled ink called SuperQuink. It was advertised as the "ink that was proper for every social situation." The ad copy went on to conclude: "So, to avoid embarrassment in your social correspondence, be sure to use Parker Super-Quink." The campaign was successful in the United States, so it was exported to the Mexican market. Twenty thousand metal signs were imprinted in Spanish with the theme ". . . to avoid embarrassment, use Parker Super-Quink." The direct translation into Spanish of the first three words is " . . . *para evitar embarazo* . . ." which is what appeared on the signs. Unfortunately, what Parker did not know is that in Mexico those words form a special idiom that translates: ". . . to avoid *pregnancy*, use Parker Super-Quink."

Many savvy international marketers revert to the use of numbers rather than words for product identification. The reason is that numbers rarely have double meanings. Perhaps best known are the commercial aircraft manufacturers with their gaggle of models in the 700 category: 707, 727, 747, 767, etc.

Parker discovered the universality of numbers in the 1930s which is one reason its famous 51 pen, launched in the fifty-first anniversary of the company, gave birth to a whole string of pen models bearing numbers instead of names: the 61, 21, 45, and so on. Since 80 percent of Parker's business is done outside the United States, naming its products has always been a carefully studied task, especially after its SuperQuink experience.

However, computer chip manufacturers have perhaps carried this numerical idea several numbers too far. In 1978, Intel Corporation introduced its 8086 chip. The following year, Motorola countered with its 68000. Intel responded with an 8088 and then an 80286.

In 1983, Motorola produced the 68010 and then a 68020. So, in 1984, Intel produced the 80286 and then the next year the 80386. This Ping-Pong game of names continues to this day.

Naming products for worldwide consumers with safe yet original names has become a commercial business within itself. When Honda wanted a new name for one of its models, it turned to a firm called Namelab in San Francisco and paid $35,000 for the word *Acura.*

One name change that hardly needed outside consultants occurred in the 1920s in Kenosha, Wisconsin, where a company there made men's underwear. The name of the company's most popular underwear style was the Kenosha Klosed Krotch. It was changed to Jockey, and now Jockey International is a world-known corporate name.

Here are other examples of problematic brand names:

- Chrysler's $200,000 production sports car was called the Diablo, but its original name was Countach, which, when pronounced in Italian, means . . . what a rude man might utter upon spying a good-looking woman.

- Unilever sells its fabric softener throughout Europe but under seven separate names, often with different bottles, different marketing strategies, and sometimes even different formulas.

- Candy maker Mars, trying to standardize its brands in Europe, killed off its successful Marathon name for a chocolate bar in favor of the name so popular in the United States, Snickers. Similarly, candies known as Bonitos in France were rebaptized M&Ms.

Americans are not alone in this business of brand names that need Band-Aids. Japan's Nissan, for example, found that its Bluebird sedan was not sexy enough for American buyers, so it was renamed Stanza. The same is true with its Fair Lady sports car, which became the 300ZX.

Other names that bombed on the American market include a French soft drink called Pschitt; the Japanese coffee creamer Creap; and a Finnish product used to unfreeze car locks called Super Piss.

Finally, perhaps the paradigm that illustrates how American business should respect global brand names involves the name Exxon. Originally known as Esso, the oil corporation changed to Exxon only after testing pronunciation of the new name in 56 languages and 113 local dialects.

In summary, selecting brand names for the international market should not be made with casual or "lite" research.

## EUROSPEAK

As the majority of European nations move, albeit haltingly, toward economic union, it is inevitable that new business lingo will become more pervasive. Here are some words and phrases selected from a European business dictionary, *Business Buzzwords, The Tough New Jargon of Modern Business,* by Michael Johnson (Basil Blackwell, 1990).

*affluenza:* Sudden, windfall affluence.

*brain candy:* Bad TV or trashy fiction.

*danegeld:* Originally, a tax paid to the Danes centuries ago; now any form of business blackmail.

*dochakuka:* Among the Japanese, the skill of adapting to local conditions.

*glocal:* From "thinking globally but acting locally." One example: Tailoring products to local tastes.

*kill:* Used as a noun to mean a sale or a deal.

*serious money:* Quantities of money sufficient to make a difference after taxes are deducted.

*synergy:* Two decades ago, it was a positive word, meaning the whole was greater than the parts. Now it is taking on negative connotations because it often suggests another agenda, such as merging in order to reduce headcounts.

*weltanschauung:* Taken from the German word, which means "world view"; it is a desirable trait in business today.

*zaitech:* A coined word from the Japanese, which means earning profits from investments rather than from sales.

To this glossary might be added:

*ECU:* An acronym, pronounced *EH-cue,* that means "European Currency Unit." One goal of the European Economic Community is to create a "European Currency Unit," or common currency. Coincidentally, in France centuries ago, there was an actual coin called an *ecu.*

*Eurobrands:* A single brand name acceptable to all European markets; what American consumer product companies would like to establish, but as we have seen earlier, local markets resist.

*Euroconsumer:* The hoped-for but maddeningly elusive pan-European consumer who will buy the identical American product sold in identical ways in every European country.

Learning this new Eurospeak might avoid major goofs and gaffes such as in the following story:

> An American automobile executive was transferred to his company's operation in the United Kingdom, where he announced to the media that the factory would soon be installing a new line of robotic assembly machines. A local reporter asked if that meant any employees would become *redundant,* which is the British term for "laid off." Unaware of that, the manager replied, "Oh, no, no, no. However, we will be *phasing out* about five hundred people."

## SUMMARY

The word *empathy* is defined as having an unspoken knowledge and appreciation for another person's feelings, beliefs, and thoughts. In business, when dealing with someone whose knowledge of American English is limited, empathy can be a valuable asset to apply to every spoken or written word.

As we have seen here, a sensitivity to our business lingo can avoid embarrassment, help insure against product failures, speed negotiations, and build rapport and trust in all types of business relationships. Learn to apply this sensitivity, and you will be converting our existing tower of business babel into a beacon of clear communication and understanding.

# 9

# Confusing Cognates
# and Telephone Talk

In this chapter, we deal with two other idiosyncrasies in languages around the world—cognates and answers to the often overlooked question, How do I answer the telephone?

We'll begin with cognates and this illustrative true story:

Stella, a lovely Mexican woman, is married to an American, and they now live in Houston where she works for the Port of Houston. "My English is good," Stella says, "but occasionally I get tripped up by Spanish words that are almost identical to English words but that have different meanings. For example, I went to the doctor several weeks ago because my head and sinuses were terribly stuffed. When he asked, 'What seems to be the problem?' I explained that my nose was constipated. After a few moments of complete confusion and then laughter, we both learned that in Spanish the word *constipado* is used for *both* conditions: congestion and constipation."

Such confusion can be found in every language.

In French, these are called *faux amis,* an apt phrase since it means "false friends." In every language, there are words that look and sound like similar words in other languages but that mean different things.

When they look or sound alike and also *mean* the same thing, they are called *cognates.* The American Heritage Dictionary defines a cognate as "(1) related by blood; having a common ancestor; (2) related in origin, as certain words in different languages derived from the same root."

Cognates can be very helpful to American "innocents abroad" who see or hear a familiar word, because suddenly a glimmer of clarity will emerge from a muddy stream of foreign words.

But, as Stella learned, some cognates can also be confusing, even confounding, and that's when they are called false cognates. In this chapter, you will be given a quick, short course in false cognates so that you can be wary of them as you converse your way around the world. They exist in almost all languages. However, for this lesson, we will list cognates from two languages—Spanish and German—because they provide some handy, amusing examples.

## SPANISH COGNATES

Spanish is one of those languages where it seems so tempting to take American words, put an *o* on them, and hope they will be correct in Spanish. Karen Lee Smith, an exporter in Fresno, California, tells about the time she did this on a selling trip into Mexico: "I wanted to say that the foodstuffs I was selling had preservatives in them, so I simply used what I hoped was the Spanish word—*preservativos.* It turned out that in Mexico that happens to be the word for condoms. Needless to say, my customer was startled and shocked. I later learned that the Spanish word for preservatives is *conservadores.*"

Stewart Skidmore was born in Cuba of American parents, raised in Mexico, and attended American schools. Consequently, he was fluent in both Spanish and American English. Yet it wasn't until his mature years that he learned that the Spanish word *moleste* was more benign than the English word *molest.* In Spanish, it merely means "to bother" someone, where in English it usually connotes accosting and harassing someone sexually.

Here are more false cognates in Spanish:

*Realizar* does not mean "to realize"; it means "to accomplish."

*Pretender* does not mean "to pretend"; it means "to try to do" something.

*Sensible* means "sensitive," and *sensato* translates to "sensible" in English.

The Spanish word *ignorar* means "to ignore facts" and not people.

*Actual* and *actualmente* do not mean "actual" or "actually"; they mean "at the present time."

*Ultamamente* does not mean "ultimately"; it means "lately."

*Asistir* does not mean "to assist"; it means "to attend."

*Borde* is not the border between two countries; it is the "edge." That word also means wild, uncultivated, and bastard, but it should not be used in place of *frontera*, which is the border (or "frontier") between two countries.

*Equipo* is not "equipment"; it is a "team."

*Equipaje* also resembles "equipment," but in Spanish it means "baggage."

This is just a partial list. The number of both true and false cognates is extensive in Spanish.


## GERMAN COGNATES

Earlier in this text, we explained that when you order a dry martini in Germany, it's entirely possible that the waiter will bring you three martinis. Reason: The German word *drie*, pronounced *dry*, is the word for "three."

Here are some more possibly dangerous cognates, as supplied by Peter Hoyng, born in Bonn, Germany, who has lived in the

United States for five years and currently studies and teaches German at a university here.

> *Sensibil* seems similar to the English word *sensible*; however, where in English it means "level-headed," in German it means "timid."
>
> The word *lust* in English almost always has a sexual connotation, but in German it is used to mean "in the mood for" as in going out to dinner, to the movies, etc.
>
> The German word *sympathisch* would seem to be related to the English word *sympathetic*; but instead of meaning "a sharing of feelings," it simply means "to like" in German.
>
> *Der test* in German means "a quiz," but the Germans also use the word *quiz* to mean a "guessing game."
>
> Germans may be heard using the English words *flipper* and *old-timer*; but for them they are used in this context: a *flipper* is a "pinball machine," and an *old-timer* is an "old car."

Incidentally, there is no such word as *roommate* in German; so they must say *mitbewohnerin*, which means "the person who lives with you."

Finally, Hoyng tells of the time his car broke down in the United States, and translating literally from the German, he phoned a mechanic to advise that his car had "broken together." It took several moments of complete confusion to repair that cross-lingual mess.

## TELEPHONE TALK

You pick up your telephone, punch in a country and city code for Mexico, and are greeted by something that sounds like *DEEGA-may*. What's going on? Not all nationalities use—or even know—our customary American telephone greeting of *Hello*. Your associate in Mexico is saying "Speak to me!" Or, in Spanish, *digame*.

Here, to paste next to your international dialing instructions, is a quick reference for the proper way people around the world say "Hello" over the telephone.

*Japan:* Here you will be greeted by a tender, sibilant sounding *mushi-mushi.*

*Russia:* Your Russian phonemate will probably begin with *slushaiyu,* meaning "I'm listening." But a more worldly Russian might say "'allo."

*Italy:* Italians use a memorable one. They say *pronto,* which means "I'm ready." Or, they may say *prego,* which means "please" or, literally, "I beg you."

*China:* Here you will hear a soft, gentle word that sounds like the English word *way.* It is actually *wei* and is repeated with a slight pause in between: "*wei . . . wei.*"

*Germany:* The custom here, especially in business, is to pick up the phone and say your last name.

What about the man who started it all? What was his preference for the first words we should speak when answering the telephone? Alexander Graham Bell thought his invention should use *Hoy! Hoy!* as a greeting. This, it is supposed, was probably because in his age the byways of communication and commerce were the seas, and how did ships at sea greet one another? Why with *Ahoy!* of course.

# 10

# How to Be Understood

In the previous nine chapters, you've learned all about the gambles of communicating around the world in American English. Now it's time to learn how to improve the odds.

## TEN TIPS FOR USING AMERICAN ENGLISH

Following are ten specific tips for communicating effectively using American English.

### Tip #1

Speak slowly and distinctly. Among international business savants, it is said you can determine who the experienced professionals are by the slow pace of their speech.

### Tip #2

Speak and write using simple syntax and vocabulary. Avoid all of the following:

- idioms ("It's raining cats and dogs.")
- slang ("We don't want any hanky panky with this business deal.")
- euphemisms ("I need to visit the restroom.")
- sports terminology ("When in doubt, drop back and punt.")
- acronyms ("We need a reservation ASAP.")
- jargon ("My PC takes CD-ROM programs.")

### Tip #3

Enunciate clearly. This means avoiding those words and contractions we Americans seem to butcher:

gonna

wanna

wouldja

oughta

shudda

comin'

goin'

whatcha

saying *ya* instead of *you*

saying *em* instead of *them*

### Tip #4

Watch the eyes. In fact, watch for all types of body language. Social scientists claim that fully 60 percent of our daily communication is nonverbal. But the eyes are especially important. Among some cultures, it is believed that the eyes are the windows of the soul. And when trying to communicate, a person's eyes will tell you much

*Watch the eyes. A person's eyes will tell you if he or she is comprehending what you're saying.*

about comprehension. The exception is among Oriental cultures, where direct eye contact is considered impolite.

If another person's eyes glaze over when you are talking, stop, retreat, and retrace your verbal steps to try to regain attention.

Other body signs to look for: a person who nods as you speak is usually comprehending, even agreeing; yet a person who thrusts out his or her chin is usually showing defiance. Also, when you are conversing, don't be afraid to be expressive with your face and hands in order to accentuate your words.

### *Tip #5*

Be careful with numbers. Write them down or repeat them. For instance, in some languages, like Japanese, numbers are stated in forms that are different from our system. In Japanese, one million is stated as "one-hundred, ten-thousands." Even without differences like that, it is easy to become confused when crossing back and forth between languages. Here is an example:

> Paul and Barb Odland were shopping in a Mexican street market when Paul spotted a carving that he wanted to buy. Since Barb was fluent in Spanish, she interpreted for Paul and the vendor. The price for the carving was 100 pesos.

With Barb interpreting, Paul offered 50 pesos. The vendor countered with 90 pesos, which Barb relayed back to Paul who then told her to offer 60. The bidding got faster and narrower, with Barb swiveling back and forth between Paul and the vendor until, suddenly, she realized they had *passed* one another! She burst into laughter and explained the problem, and Paul and the vendor quickly, but sheepishly, agreed on a final price.

### Tip #6

Never assume that people around you do not understand English. For instance, it's tempting, when in a public setting such as riding on public transportation, to assume that because you do not hear any English that your fellow passengers do not comprehend it. In situations like this, Americans are often guilty of making critical remarks about the locale, living conditions, the conveyance, or even the local people. However, it's entirely possible that someone within earshot is fluent in English.

### Tip #7

Try to learn some phrases in the language of the country you plan to visit. The Appendix in this book provides insights into six different languages, plus it supplies a handful of handy phrases. Americans who have studied and learned another language have acquired a sense for how difficult it can be trying to communicate using unfamiliar rules for grammar and pronunciation. They know how easy it is to make mistakes in verb tenses. Therefore, just making an attempt to speak a few phrases from the country you are visiting is a footbridge to creating good personal relationships. It's good to *parlez*, but there are also limits. Don't assume your three years of high school French qualify you to speak fluently, especially when conducting business. You might end up giving the whole store away.

### Tip #8

Use visual aids wherever possible. For example, if you are unable to get someone to understand a key word, point to it in the dictionary.

If you are asking directions, use a map to trace the route rather than rely on verbal instructions. If necessary, play charades to help make your point or illustrate your question.

### Tip #9

Avoid anything that may dull your senses and your awareness level. A glass of wine may help you relax, lose inhibitions, and become a bit more communicative; but a whole bottle will not necessarily make you instantly fluent in some new language or more easily understood by a non-native student of English. It's more likely to merely cause static in your receptors. When traveling and communicating abroad, the object is to avoid misunderstandings.

### Tip #10

Finally, summarize, paraphrase, and echo. Repeat what you are saying and hearing, using different terms. One diplomatic device is to say, "I know that sometimes I speak very fast. Perhaps it would be helpful to stop and review, in your words, what we have discussed."

These ten tips will help you improve communications significantly, whether you are a tourist, student, or businessperson traveling abroad.

## OTHER WAYS TO COMMUNICATE

Bear in mind, too, that communicating is a two-way street. Listening is half of the equation. In fact, a University of Minnesota study indicated that fully 60 percent of all misunderstandings come from poor listening.

Also, we communicate verbally, using body language and gestures, but also by other means: protocol, etiquette, comportment—however you choose to describe *behavior*—each of these can communicate volumes about you. Take silence, for example. Americans don't like silence. If a few seconds of silence occur during a business conference or a social conversation, someone usually jumps in to say something. In other cultures, however, silence can truly be "golden." Among the Japanese, there may be long periods (long by American standards) where nothing is said. For example:

> A North Carolina lawyer relates how he once accompanied a client to Japan to make a business proposal to potential customers there. The client presented his case to the Japanese and then sat back to hear reactions. Instead, he was met with silence. Not realizing this was a normal Japanese custom, he interpreted it to mean disinterest, even rejection. So, the American moved on to his alternate, back-up proposal . . . revealing concessions without realizing that the silence merely meant the Japanese were still contemplating the first offer.

## COLORS COMMUNICATE TOO

In American culture, certain colors send certain messages. Black is considered morbid, dark, and mysterious. In fact, one of our allusions is to "white hats" (the good guys) and "black hats" (the bad guys.) Red suggests exuberance, energy, and even rage. Green and blue are "cool" colors, or are associated with the environment. Green also symbolizes jealously. Pink is considered feminine. And so it goes.

The same is true outside the United States—same in the sense that colors convey messages, but not necessarily the same messages. For example:

- Green is the national color of Egypt, but it should not be used for packages.

- The French, Dutch, and Swedes associate green with cosmetics and toiletries.

- In the Orient, green suggests exuberance, but when agriculturalist Steve Renk visited northern China and distributed green baseball caps, he found that men refused to wear them.

The reason? In that region, when a man wore a green hat, it advertised that his wife or sister was a prostitute.

- Purple is the color of death and funerals in Brazil and Mexico. And yellow marigolds are the cemetery flower in Mexico, meaning they are presented only for decorations at cemeteries.

- White is the color of death and rebirth in Japan, so it may be seen at both funerals and weddings.

- In the Orient, bright red envelopes are used to present gifts of money.

- White can represent purity and is therefore the predominant color in the United States for wedding dresses; however, in India, bright red or yellow fabrics are preferred.

## THE MEANING OF NUMBERS

Laura B. lived in Japan as a young girl because her father, an American, had been assigned there by his American employer. Laura had a young Japanese girl named Miko as a live-in companion. On the occasion of her mother's birthday, Laura's father presented her mother with a beautiful ring decorated with four exquisite pearls. When Miko saw the gift, she turned white and explained, "You must not accept that. Four is an unlucky number. It means death." Laura's family smiled and brushed off Miko's advice. Several days later, they found the ring was missing one of its pearls. When they asked Miko, she confessed that she had removed it because she simply could not allow Laura's mother to wear such a deadly omen.

This true story dramatizes how powerful some superstitions can be among some cultures. In Japan, as well as in China and Korea, the word *shi* means "four," but it also means "death." So, among Orientals, the relationship between the two meanings is strong.

At the opposite end of the superstition scale stands the number eight. In the Orient, the word for eight is pronounced *faat*, which also means "to prosper." There are eight emblems in both Confucianism and Buddhism. Author Angi Ma Wong, who is also a marketing consultant in California, explains that many Chinese businesses flock to the San Gabriel Valley of southern California because the area code there is 818.

Among the Chinese, *gow* is the word for nine and is popular because it is associated with dragons and longevity. In Japan, however, the number nine is associated with suffering, so it has bad symbolism there.

Throughout much of Europe, as in the United States, the number thirteen represents bad luck. And when presenting flowers in Europe, always give an odd number of blooms (but not thirteen), because an even number is considered unlucky.

If you consider this strange, remember that many Christians in the United States recoil at the number 666, since it is widely believed to represent the Devil.

Finally, bear in mind that even the numbers on our calendar are not necessarily followed universally. In the Moslem world, a separate calendar is kept based on the birth of the prophet Mohammed. And in the Orient, the Lunar calendar dictates when one of the most celebrated holidays is held, the Chinese New Year.

## OTHER WAYS TO *COMPRENDER*

The ultimate way to be understood while in another country is to learn the other person's language.

This is easier said than done and could involve years and years of study. Americans have a special dilemma, because we don't know which language to learn. You could spend a lifetime learning, say, Portuguese and then, except for a vacation or two, find that your travels take you to places where Portuguese is not spoken.

Still, the best argument for at least trying to learn a different language is the one presented elsewhere in this book: that trying to learn another language makes us more understanding and sympathetic when dealing with people struggling to speak American English.

There are four levels of achievement when learning another language:

1. The one-hundred-word level, where you can say and understand a basic minimum vocabulary. However, at this rudimentary level, you can easily miss 98 percent of what is going on around you. Still, it's better than nothing.

2. The social or "courtesy" level, where you can meet and greet people, ask directions, and converse at about the level of a three- or four-year-old.

3. The "survival" level, where you could spend extensive time in another country and communicate and comprehend much of what goes on around you.

4. The near fluency level, where you can work and socialize with proficiency.

For myself, after 35 years in international business and after considerable home and classroom study of French and Spanish, I have never reached that fourth level. I am convinced the only way I could ever achieve it would be to spend, say, a full six months living in the country of choice. Therefore, in my opinion, nothing can replace living every hour of each day where you are forced to communicate in that new language.

Levels one, two, and three, on the other hand, are reachable for many Americans. To achieve them, here are some resources to consider:

- Berlitz and similar professional language schools offer excellent instruction, ranging from weekly classes to the "total immersion" system. In the latter, you devote anywhere from one to six weeks and spend all your waking hours learning, talking, and trying to think in another language. Information about Berlitz courses can be obtained by calling 1-800-923-7548. For other language schools in your area, consult the Yellow Pages in your telephone directory.

- Language/30 tape cassette system offers thirty different languages taught by a self-learning method. It is based on the U.S. military "speed-up" language learning method developed for U.S. government personnel preparing for overseas duty. Each course is comprised of two audiocassettes, a phrase dictionary, and a handy carrying case. These cassettes are available in bookstores and in selected mail-order catalogs.

- Check with your local community college to learn what language courses are available in your community.

- Living Language Basic Course is for beginners or those wanting a refresher course. It uses three hours of recordings, accompanied by a conversation manual and dictionary. It is available in retail stores or by calling 1-800-733-3000.

- Accelerated Learning Techniques claims it can teach you one of eight different languages and have you conversing comfortably in thirty days. The cost is around $300, and the program comes with cassettes and other learning materials.

A warning, however. John Ratliff, president of Diplomatic Language Services in Arlington, Virginia, says that Americans' expectations are too high and that we don't realize how difficult another language can be. Consequently, we tend to think we can learn a language faster than it actually requires.

Whether its numbers, colors, superstitions, or holidays, each can be a comfortable conversational gambit to help you learn more about conversing across cultures.

# Words about Words

Sometime in the next decade, you will reach into your pocket, remove your four-ounce, flip-top cellular telephone, and punch in a series of digits. Those signals will be bounced off a ring of satellites circling the earth and connect you with any point on the globe. The result: Instant communication. No problem.

However, the problems begin, as I have demonstrated in this book, the moment your *words* pass through the ether regions. Communication improves while the opportunity for miscommunication expands.

In the Introduction to this book, I cited a *USA Today* survey that indicated the greatest fear for people traveling outside the United States was the inability to communicate. If you were among that concerned majority, I hope the contents of this book have helped reduce that apprehension. I hope you have acquired a new awareness, a new sensitivity for our American dialect and how it must be treated gingerly around the world in order to communicate more effectively.

In a single phrase, I hope you have developed a new respect for the world of words . . . and especially for English words.

If so, it seems appropriate to conclude this text with some provocative words about words. Accordingly, here are some apt quotations from the ages about the role of words in our global community.

Actions speak louder than words.
> —Abraham Lincoln, 1856

Evil communications corrupt good manners.
> —The First Epistle of Paul the
> Apostle to the Corinthians, 15:33

Words are the clothes that thoughts wear—only the clothes.
> —English author Samuel Butler
> (1835–1902)

Words like winter snowflakes.
> —The Iliad

I still live.
> —Last words of Daniel Webster,
> October 24, 1852

Nothing is more common than for men to think that because they are familiar with words they understand the ideas they stand for.
> —Cardinal John Newman
> (1801–1890)

Some guy hit my fender the other day and I said unto him, "Be fruitful and multiply," but not in those words.
> —Woody Allen

How often misused words generate misleading thoughts.
> —Herbert Spencer

Language is thinking, and thinking is language, and the rest is silence.
>                    —Ludwig Wittgenstein

Modern man . . . is educated to understand foreign languages and misunderstand foreigners.
>                    —English author G. K. Chesterton
>                    (1874–1936)

# Appendix

# What to Know
# about Other Languages and
# Cultures

*Senator Paul Simon (D-Ill.) is so troubled by America's monolingualism that he claims we should erect signs at all our international airports to greet arrivals from overseas. According to Simon, those signs should say:* Welcome to America. We do not speak your language.

The American attitude about learning other languages was best captured by the satirist H. L. Mencken: "If English was good enough for Jesus Christ, it's good enough for me."

In defense of such xenophobia, Americans have little need to learn other languages because our own country is so vast, and also because so many other cultures are taking the effort to learn ours. In addition, there is the vexing question, Which one of the dozen or more popular languages should we learn?

The counterargument, as expressed elsewhere in this book, is that Americans should study other languages because they open new worlds and new opportunities for communication. Also, studying another language brings an automatic appreciation for how easy it is to make mistakes; it makes us more tolerant and forgiving when those trying to speak English stumble and struggle.

Another strong argument for learning another language is, as cross-cultural trainer James Bostain reminds us: "We must remember that 95 percent of the rest of the world is un-American."

When traveling abroad, encountering another language is like walking past an untended Nintendo game—there is always that impulse to poke a few buttons and play the game just to see how far one can progress up the ladder of comprehension.

If you should decide to poke a few language buttons, one piece of advice comes from author Kenneth B. Morgan. In his lighthearted guide to world travel *Speaking You English?* (Morrow, 1973), Morgan argues that the secret to linguistic survival is to shun the grammar, irregular verb forms, and masculinity or femininity of words. Rather, he argues, the secret for quick communication is to learn just *nouns*.

As evidence, Morgan points to infants. They communicate quite effectively with a limited vocabulary comprised almost totally of nouns: ice cream, toy, bunny, doggie, momma, daddy, cookie, and so on.

Also, Morgan explains, as another helpful aspect, that Portuguese-speaking people can usually understand Spanish, the Dutch understand German, and almost all Scandinavians understand Swedish. Morgan's point is that if we concentrate on learning a few critical nouns in just a few languages, we can cope fairly well. For example, Morgan says that in English, French, or German, the following "tourist nouns" are the same, with minor variations: *taxi, cigarette, police, whiskey, restaurant,* and *hotel.* And let's not forget the ubiquitous *no.* That's very similar in lots of languages.

Whether one decides to make a major commitment to learn another language, or whether one merely wishes a nodding acquaintanceship with other languages, this section is intended to help you "shake hands" with six of the world's more popular languages.

In the sections that follow, you will learn more twists and tricks to help you move more comfortably around our "spaceship" Earth—facts about each language from people who know firsthand what it's like to cope in a second language.

I am indebted to Maria Meyer-Nettum for her extensive research in collecting material for this section. Maria is a graduate of the University of Wisconsin School of Mass Communication, and she spent the better part of a year researching, interviewing, and assembling information. The University of Wisconsin (at Madison) boasts one of the largest populations of international students in the country and teaches over 140 different languages, so Maria was able to mine a rich lode of information. Maria speaks fluent Spanish and is also a flight attendant for an international airline; therefore, she was able to interview a wide selection of international travelers, asking for advice and experiences in traversing language borders.

Also, the translations and phonetic spellings at the end of each language section were provided courtesy of AD HOC Translations Inc., 611 Broadway, Suite 803, New York, NY 10012; Phone (212) 979-2816; FAX (212) 505-1998.

## JAPANESE

As with many other languages, you already know a smattering of Japanese. We Americans have adopted Japanese words like *kimono, sake, samurai, sukiyaki, hari kari, sumo* (as in *sumo wrestling*), and *tsunami.*

The Japanese have also adopted countless English words. Just a few of them are *post, ball, bus, pool, automation, rush, merit,* and *television.*

Before we get too comfortable, however, some of these loanwords can get a bit slippery. For example, we use the Japanese word *hibachi,* but in Japan it does not refer to a small barbecue grill, although it's close—it refers to a large porcelain pot with burning charcoal used for warmth in a Japanese home.

Borrowing loanwords has become something of a fad among the Japanese young, trendy generation. Even then, misunderstandings pop up. For example, what the Japanese call a *trainer* is a "sweatshirt" to an American. *Freeze* to a Japanese means "ice cream." A *health meter* to a Japanese is a "scale" to us. In Japanese grocery stores, you can buy *Creap,* which is a coffee creamer. And on the container for a nose decongestant were printed these words: *For stuffed noses and snot.*

English is widely studied in Japan, thanks to people like the late Herman Kahn, futurist and founder of the famous Hudson Institute. In the 1960s, Kahn was hired by the Japanese government to advise the Japanese on how to become more integrated into the world economy. One step he recommended was to teach more English. With typical Japanese dedication, it was then mandated that English should be taught in all Japanese schools. As a result, today many Japanese study English for six years before graduating from their equivalent of high school. The problem, however, is that they can read and write English but are usually very uncomfortable trying to speak English.

Because they don't use our alphabet, written Japanese is incomprehensible to Westerners. The basis for written Japanese was borrowed from the Chinese in the sixth century A.D. The Japanese writing system is called *kanji*, and, stated simply, it is a collection of small stylized pictures that represent a thing or idea. A single *kanji* character can consist of one stroke or as many as thirty strokes.

Converting these picture symbols, or ideographs, into spoken words involved changing forty-six *kanji* characters into sounds or syllables, collectively called *hiragana*. In addition, a second set of syllables was developed for words that are of Japanese origin or that came from foreign sources—this is called *katakana*. These two "sounding systems" are used by the Japanese when they wish to "spell out" words syllabically. *Katakana* also permits the thousands and thousands of *kanji* symbols to be converted by word processors into typewritten form.

Memorizing the meaning of *kanji* symbols can be daunting to outsiders because to be considered literate, you must know about two thousand of them. There are seven thousand in a commonly used dictionary, and thousands more are used by scholars.

The pronunciation of Japanese words is an easier task. There are only five basic vowel sounds in Japanese, and consonants are similar to those used in English.

The Japanese language does not differentiate between the sounds of *l* and *r*; as a result, they are often mixed when the Japanese try to speak English. *Rice* comes out sounding like *lice* and *red* like *led*, . . . which provides American comedians and other mimics with instant Japanese-sounding accents. The Japanese also have great difficulty learning to pronounce the *th* sound in English.

When communicating with the Japanese, language is only half the battle. What is left *unsaid* is equally important and can be demonstrated with the three examples that follow.

### Silence . . . Twins . . . Yes

To understand unspoken Japanese, keep those three words in mind.

First, there will be periods of *silence* in any dialogue with the Japanese. We Americans think silence is bad. Observe for yourself: When a short period of silence descends on two or more Americans at a business meeting or social gathering, someone will usually jump in and say something.

Not so with the Japanese. There may be frequent periods of silence. But that doesn't mean there isn't a stream of communication flowing back and forth. As author Robert J. Collins says, ". . . waves of feedback and information [are] flowing from stomach to stomach as the result of subtle twitchings, purrs of content or disagreement, sudden inrushes of air through clenched teeth, and the assumption of various poses (as in the pose of being asleep or the pose of being awake)."

Next, what about this business of *twins*? It derives from social anthropologist Edward T. Hall's observations that the Japanese are *highly contextual* in their communication. That means they can communicate as twin siblings might—instinctively, intuitively, without having to express it. Americans, on the other hand, are *low-context communicators*, which means we must spell out everything, every dotted *i* and comma. Could this explain why there are so many lawyers in the United States and so few in Japan?

Finally, the word *yes* is perhaps heard more frequently in Japan than any other single word. The Japanese word for "yes" is *hai*, pronounced exactly like our abbreviated form of the word *hello* which is, of course, *hi!*

It is imperative for Americans to understand that this word, *hai* or "yes," does not mean "yes." Among the Japanese, it merely serves as an acknowledgment, as in *Yes, I hear you.* But it does not mean *Yes, I agree with you.* The best catchphrase for remembering this is found in Japan expert Robert T. Moran's book, *Getting Your Yen's Worth* (Gulf Publishing, 1985). In this book on how to negotiate in business with the Japanese, Moran has an entire chapter entitled "Never Take 'Yes' for an Answer."

The overarching significance of these three terms is that they are a reflection of the Japanese society and life.

*Yes* is important because it generates harmony. *No* is rarely expressed because it would hurt too many feelings. That doesn't mean the Japanese cannot say no—they just say it in a dozen different, muffled ways. For example, *Oh, that would be very difficult* is usually a pretty clear indication of no. Another signal is a sudden intake of breath between the teeth. But an outright no would embarrass both you and the Japanese speaker, and that would be impolite in a country where politeness and respect are as important as freedom and independence are in the United States.

As an example of how respect plays an important role in both Japanese society and language, consider this. Writer Aaron Hoopes explains that to say "the child goes," one would use the Japanese verb *iku*. But, to say "the woman goes," requires a higher degree of respect, so the verb changes to *ikimasu*. And, because teachers are held in the highest respect, to say "the teacher goes" requires yet a different, even more respectful verb form, *ikaremasu*.

## Rules for Communicating with the Japanese

Here are some basic rules to remember when communicating with the Japanese:

- Ease into business discussions slowly. It may take what seems like an inordinately long time to get around to the main topic, but be patient.

- Don't be dogmatic, declarative, or overly direct. That is considered rude.

- Don't be upset by vague and indirect replies or delays. A period must elapse where mutual respect develops.

- Always speak in a moderate tone. Loud, boisterous behavior is appropriate only during drinking sessions at a nightclub.

- Watch your posture and body language. Slouching or placing your feet on furniture is considered very impolite. Also, avoid slapping someone on the back or giving an arm hug as if you were congratulating a teammate in America.

- Don't use first names; use titles instead. Also, teachers are respected in Japan and addressed as *sensei*.

- Try to phrase your questions so that they allow an affirmative answer.

A few final tips. In a country where politeness is paramount, it would be wise to memorize these three words:

*Dozo*, pronounced *DOH-zoh*, means "Please."

*Arigato*, pronounced *ahr-EE-ghat-toh*, means "Thank you."

*Sumimasen*, pronounced *suh-mee-mah-sen*, is a humble expression apologizing for any bother you may have caused . . . even when you didn't cause any bother.

When dining or being entertained, the standard toast in Japan is *Kampai!* which means "Cheers!"

Here are some useful Japanese words and phrases you can learn easily:

| | |
|---|---|
| please | *DOH-zoh* |
| thank you | *ahr-EE-ghat-toh* |
| good morning | *oh-HIY-oh go-zy-ee-mah-su* |
| good afternoon | *koh-NEE-CHEE-wah* |
| good evening | *kohn-bahn-way* |
| Where is . . .? | *. . . DO koh-des-kah* |
| bathroom | *ot-tay-AH-ry* |
| yes | *hi!* |
| no | *EEE-eh* |
| Help! | *Ta-skeh-teh!* |
| very good/well | *YO-ku-day-kee-mash-tah* |

Lastly, if you've ever visited Italy or dined with Italians, you may have heard the toast *Chin-chin*. In Japan, however, that is the term for a boy's penis (literally, his "pee-pee"). One Japanese gentleman told me when he first heard that term used as an Italian toast, his thought was, Well, we usually toast one's health, but if you want to toast my penis, it's O.K. with me.

There are many fine books on the market dealing with Japan and the Japanese language. Here are a few I have found especially helpful:

*UPDATE Japan*, by Aaron Hoopes (Intercultural Press, 1992).

*Japan-Think Ameri-Think*, by Robert J. Collins (Penguin Books, 1992).

*Getting Your Yen's Worth: How to Negotiate with Japan, Inc.*, by Robert T. Moran (Gulf Publishing, 1985).

*The Japan of Today* (The International Society for Educational Information, Inc., Tokyo, 1989).

## GERMAN

Peggy L. is an American businesswoman and president of a successful high-tech company located in the Middle West. She speaks near fluent German. Last year, while traveling in Germany, she served as interpreter for her husband, the chairman of their company. They were discussing a purchase agreement with potential customers for their product and, in the course of conversation, her husband said, "We want a written contract so that neither of us gets screwed." Peggy stopped the translation immediately, turned, and whispered to him, "Wait. My German is pretty good, and I know how to *f - - - in German, but I don't know how to get screwed.*"

Later, after they had returned to the United States, Peggy was at a dinner sponsored by the local university. By chance, at her table were two professors of German, so she inquired if they could advise what the German expression was for *to get screwed.* After ten minutes of discussion, the professors finally agreed that the German words would be *to get s - - t upon.*

This true-life example typifies the problems of translating slang into *any* language. But it seems that German is particularly susceptible to such mix-ups.

The following example, this time involving a German trying to cope with American English, was reported by syndicated travel writer Peter S. Greenberg:

A 24-year-old German student was returning home from a two-week vacation in Florida. Since he was apprehensive about flying, he quieted his nerves with a few beers before boarding the aircraft. Shortly after takeoff, he got up to go to the bathroom. Because the seat belt sign was still on, the flight attendant told him to return to his seat. The student, trying to explain his predicament, said in his fractured but forceful English, "If I don't go, it explodes!" and pushed past the attendant and went into the bathroom. You can guess the rest: the attendant reported the incident to the captain; the pilot jettisoned most of the fuel and made an emergency landing back in Florida; and the student was taken into federal custody where he remained for ten months.

Daniel J. Carlin was born in Germany, the son of a U.S. Air Force officer, who later himself became an Air Force pilot. As a result, he is fluent in both English and German. Carlin cautions Americans about translating phrases or sentences literally, because they could find themselves in embarrassing situations. He cites these examples:

- Americans say "I take a shower," which literally translated would cause a German to ask, "Where are you taking it (the shower)?" In correct German, the English phrase *I take a shower* translates to *I must me shower*.

- The German phrase *Ich mag dich* means "I like you" but be careful. In the right context, it can also mean "I *want* you."

- If a room is excessively warm, an American might say "I am hot," and the literal German translation is *Ich bin heiss*. However, for Germans this translates as "I am horny" or "I am ready."

As for more insights into German, here are some fundamentals you should know:

1. There are three genders for German nouns: masculine, feminine, and neuter.

2. Compound nouns can be formed in German. This may be why there seems to be excessively long words that appear untranslatable.

3. In English, the order in which words are placed in a sentence is much different than in German. This causes German students of American English many problems and could result in them saying in English, for example, "Throw me down the stairs my shoes."

4. Another problem for Germans learning English is our inconsistent spelling. "Spelling in English requires a good memory," says Peter Hoyng, a graduate student in the Department of German at the University of Wisconsin.

5. English is compulsory in most German schools, and because there is also a fifty-year history of military occupation by American and British soldiers, many Germans are able to speak at least some English.

6. In the eastern part of Germany, English is not as prevalent. The *Sachsen* (Saxon) dialect of German, along with Russian, is used in what was formerly East Germany.

7. In Europe, German is the most frequently spoken language (after Russian) with some ninety-five million people consider-

ing it their mother tongue. Besides Germany, German is also spoken throughout Austria and in major parts of Switzerland.

8.  Americans should realize that the German they have learned in U.S. high schools is understood, but because regional dialects vary, our "school German" is not common.

Whereas a French menu may read and sound like poetry, when it comes to foodstuffs, German is regarded by many as a most unattractive sounding language. Travel writer Bill Bryson observes that if you want whipped cream on your coffee, you order it *mit schlag*. Bryson asks, "Now does that sound to you like a frothy and delicious pick-me-up, or does that sound like the sort of thing smokers bring up first thing in the morning?"

Other German foodstuffs that Bryson says sound unappetizing include *Knoblauchbrot, Schweinskotelett ihrer Wahl*, and *Portion Schlagobers*.

Another set of colorful word concoctions might be found on German highways. According to a Munich newspaper, if you call a traffic officer a *Stinkstiefel* (meaning "smelly boot"), you could get fined about $50. But there are worse terms and higher fines: Calling the officer a *Depp* ("idiot") brings a fine in excess of $500. Call the officer a *Raubritter* ("robber baron"), and the fine is over $1,000. Topping the list would be *damischer Bullen* (or "stupid bull"), which would cost you about $1,700.

On the subject of name-calling, the American custom of quickly calling people by their first name makes Germans acutely uncomfortable. Germans always use the formal titles (for example, *Herr* for "Mr.") with both subordinates and superiors, and especially if someone is senior to you in age. Only close friends dare use first names.

In all your communication with Germans, it is good to remember that good manners are both expected and respected throughou Germany.

Edward T. Hall, famed anthropologist, observes that "languag is a direct reflection of culture and German is no exception. Just the verb often comes at the end of a German sentence, it takes while for Germans to get to the point." He advises Americans to patient and wait for Germans to make their point. Also, Americ

should follow suit and repeat key points at the end of their presentations.

Germans respect honesty and directness, according to Hall. He also advises Americans to use examples when making a point or a presentation. Turning the tables, Germans believe Americans tend to exaggerate and often resort to puffery. As a general rule, Germans avoid overstatement. For a penetrating examination of the German culture, read *Understanding Cultural Differences, Germans, French and Americans,* by Edward T. Hall and Mildred Reed Hall (Intercultural Press, 1990).

In business presentations, it is always best to provide written materials in both languages, with technical terms carefully translated and measurements and other figures converted to metric.

"Get to your point politely, and know your subject well," advises Nessa P. Loewenthal, author of *Update Germany* (Intercultural Press, 1990). The social chitchat preferred by Latins, French, and Italians is not required in Germany.

Here are some "survival" words and phrases you should know in German:

| please | *BIT-ah* |
| thank you | *DON-ka* |
| good morning | *GOO-ten MORE-ghen* |
| good afternoon | *GOO-ten TAHK* |
| good evening | *GOO-ten AH-bent* |
| good night | *GOO-tah NAH-kt* |
| Where is . . .? | *VOH iss . . .?* |
| bathroom | *twah-LET-ah* |
| yes | *ya* |
| no | *nyn* |
| Help! | *HIL-fah!* |
| very good/well | *zayr GOOT* |

## FRENCH

Don Ryan is a successful midwestern businessman who purchased and renovated a small retirement/vacation home north of Marseille in France. He has studied French for several years but still quickly apologizes for his faulty grammar and pronunciation. Accordingly, once when he entered a Parisian drugstore, he approached the druggist and began, *"Je regrette, mais je ne parle pas Français"* ("I am sorry, but I do not speak French"). The very Gallic druggist dipped his head, looked over his spectacles, sighed, and replied in perfect English, "That's quite all right. No one is perfect."

That single piece of dialogue helps describe the French attitude toward their language. In one word, *pride*; but we might warn in some sectors it is almost a "militant" pride.

Gilles Bousquet teaches French at the University of Wisconsin and is from Aix-en-Provence in southern France. "Americans who go to France and try to use their instant phrase books will probably be cut off most of the time by the French," he advises. "The French would rather talk to Americans in English—even if their English is not good—rather than hear their own language destroyed." "The French are not at all tolerant of attempts," Bousquet explains. "Only if one's French has been learned formally should he or she attempt to use it extensively while in France."

Other Francophiles advise that this is especially true in Paris and its environs. In the countryside, however, people tend to be more tolerant and understanding when visitors try to speak their language.

The first tip to carry with you, then, is to understand that, above all other cultures, the French are probably the most nationalistic when it comes to language.

The French believe it is especially important to retain the purity of their language. They want it used properly, and they particularly resent the incursion of English words into their everyday vocabulary—which, when it happens, is labeled *Franglais*, meaning the combination of French and English. Indeed, at one point, the French government wanted to make it a crime to use such non-French words as *weekend* or *drugstore*. Those French purists seem to be fighting a rear guard action, however. The younger generation there, fed on a steady diet of American music videos, movies, and

CNN, prefers to call a *sandwich* exactly that, rather than the literal French, which would be *deux morceaux de pain avec quelque chose au milieu* ("two pieces of bread with something in the middle"). Other examples of frowned-upon *Franglais*: *Le weekend* is when Mom and Dad don *les tennis* and go for *un jogging, un footing,* or a *match de foot* ("soccer").

The second tip is that if you attempt a few French words and phrases, be prepared to be corrected, even put down. Don't be dismayed. Many French people are flattered that you will at least try to speak their language. This is especially true of young people and some business people who are struggling to learn American English. In some lucky cases, such a mutual struggle creates a bonding force.

Above all, French is a beautiful language, and in their spirited conversations, the French enjoy sincere debate, tests of logic, and witticisms. As one Francophile says, "Like the French opera, even a French menu can be an expression of poetry."

Here are some more specific tips to carry with you when visiting French-speaking areas:

- France's population is about fifty-five million, but French is also the principal language in adjacent Belgium and Switzerland. (Bear in mind, however, that in Belgium, French is one of two official languages, the other being Flemish; and in Switzerland, there are four official languages: French, Italian, German, and Romanche.) French is also spoken in Quebec province in Canada, parts of West Africa, Mauritius, Madagascar, Morocco, parts of the West Indies (Guadeloupe, Martinique, and Haiti), French Guiana (in South America), and Vietnam and Cambodia (in Southeast Asia).

- When meeting someone, don't jump to the use of his or her first name. Use the equivalent of *Mr., Mrs.,* or *Miss* (which are *Monsieur, Madame,* and *Mademoiselle*). While the younger generation may move quickly to first names, it is generally best to wait to be invited to use given names. Therefore, when greeting someone, the proper phrase is *Bonjour* ("Good day") *Monsieur,* or *Madame* or *Mademoiselle*.

- Two French persons, when carrying on a discussion, may interrupt one another, raise their voices, and use expressive gestures. While this may sound like aggressive behavior, it is the norm there.

- Like German and Spanish, the French have two ways of addressing one another. The English pronoun *you* is expressed either in a formal sense or in a familiar sense. It also means that verbs have different endings, depending on if the formal or familiar pronoun is used.

- Shaking hands is done more often than in the United States. The French will shake hands when arriving and leaving; they do it each and every time there is an encounter. Failing to shake hands is considered rude.

- Close friends will kiss cheeks (once, twice, sometimes even three times); however, it is more a brushing of cheeks than a true smacker. Two men, however, rarely do so.

- By American standards, business letter-writing among the French uses flowery language. Also, verbal agreements should always be followed by a formal written agreement.

- Among the most common mistakes when trying to speak French is expressing one's age. In English, we say one *is* so many years old; in French, one *has* an age.

- According to anthropologist Edward T. Hall, the French are "eloquent and relish conversation." Furthermore, because they are "high-context communicators [they] will often talk around the point they wish to make and sometimes the listener must be intuitive to discover the hidden message that is being communicated."

- The French sometimes dislike the American custom of getting right down to business. Therefore, it might be better to allow for an introductory period of social, informal conversation before jumping into business discussions. Also, avoid discussing business at the beginning of a meal; wait until the fruit and cheese course or until your French counterparts introduce business topics.

- As with all languages, there are tricky idioms. For example, a student of French might automatically think that to say "I am full" after eating a big meal would be *Je suis plein*. While *plein* does mean "full," in this case the meaning is "I am a pregnant animal."

- French is one of those languages where nouns are either masculine or feminine, and each has a separate article preceding it. For example, *la pipe* (feminine) means "the pipe," but *le pipe* (masculine) means "the penis."

Some useful words and phrases in French are as follows:

| | |
|---|---|
| please | *sihl-vhoo-play* |
| thank you | *mare-SEE* |
| good day | *bohn-JHOOR* |
| good evening | *bohn-SWAR* |
| good night | *bun-NWEE* |
| Where is . . .? | *OU ay . . .?* |
| bathroom | *twah-LET* |
| hotel | *oh-TELL* |
| yes | *wee* |
| no | *noh* |
| Help! | *Oh-skhoor!* |
| very good/well | *tray bee-YEN/bohn* |

Finally, two French words that cause Americans confusion when it comes to hotels and personal hygiene are *bidet* and *douche*. A *bidet* is a bathroom fixture, which, at first glance, resembles a toilet bowl. However, close inspection will show that it has hot and cold water faucets and a spigot that sprays water upward. It is used to clean the genitals. The word *douche* is the French word for the type of shower customarily found in American bathrooms, complete with showerhead and shower curtain or door.

# ITALIAN

An American businessman, Denis D., writes: "I recently left as vice president and general manager of a multimillion-dollar-sales, Italian-owned company after seven years. The Italian owners spoke no English, I spoke no Italian, and by the time we sorted out what the other wanted and how it was to be done, we found we didn't like each other."

A pity . . . and a valuable language lesson, all in one. A pity because each side failed to at least try to learn the other's language, and a lesson because it shows how essential good cross-cultural communication can be in both business and human relationships.

When visiting Italy, learning at least a bit of the language is well worth the effort if only because Italians appear to have so much fun speaking their language. Accompanied by an infinite number of facial expressions, hand gestures, laughs, and exclamations, the Italian language is like a full orchestra of communication.

Italians can also be wonderfully hospitable to visitors, whether you are cycling in Tuscany or boating in Venice. As Hugh Shankland, a lecturer in Italian studies, says: "Italians are used to foreigners: invading armies of the past, armies of tourists today. Eight million people visit Venice each year, and there are only 75,000 Venetians."

Hospitality is a Mediterranean tradition. Then, add a history of international trade and business, and Italy becomes a wonderful place to visit and do business. "Spontaneous courtesy and agreeable informality characterize most Italians' direct dealings with outsiders," writes Shankland.

Americans who visit Italy are aided by several facts: first, English is taught in Italian schools; second, knowing English is considered an asset to a business career; third, English is popular among young people because of movies, TV, and music; and lastly, Americans liberated Italy in the 1940s.

This does not mean English is spoken extensively. Even with their extrovertish nature, Italians—like Americans—seem to rebel when it comes to learning other languages.

Enrico Pochettino, who was born and raised near Rome, is the owner of an Italian restaurant. Here's how he rates American English in terms of difficulty: American idioms and slang are merely "a learning experience" and can usually be understood in the context of the sentence or thoughts. Grammar is not a serious problem because Italian can be even more complex. However, the pronunciation of American English words definitely causes the biggest headache. And, because spelling and pronunciation *should* go hand-in-hand (although in American English they seem to be two *separate* hands), the second most difficult problem is just that, spelling.

Robin Worth, an American graduate student in French and Italian, lived in Italy for one year. The problem she encountered was when she heard Italians utter a *tsk-tsk-tsk* sound, as when Americans indicate *shame-shame-shame*. Whenever she heard this sound, Worth thought she had committed some major *faux pas* and was being reprimanded for it. She later learned that in Italy this simply means no, without any other ramifications.

Another problem for Worth was that when she was nervous or anxious, she would think in English and speak in Italian. To voice enthusiasm, Worth would say things like "I am excited about going to Milano for the weekend." In Italian, *eccitato* means "excited" but only in the sexual sense. Looking back, Worth now remembers how many raised eyebrows she caused when talking about being "excited" about some course of action.

Here are some other gems of information you should know about Italian:

- *Prego* is a wonderful Italian word that you will hear often. It can mean "please," "you're welcome," or "go right ahead." Literally, it means "I beg you." But when answering the phone Italians usually say *pronto*.

- *Ciao* may be heard in trendy New York or Beverly Hills, but in Italy you say it only to people whom you know well enough to use the familiar form of *you*. Otherwise it is proper to say *buongiorno* ("good day") or *arrivederci* ("good-bye").

- *Pasta*, which is used in both Italian and American English, means "dough"; but in Italy, there are more than three hundred different shapes, and each region has its own favorites.

- When dining, for a change of pace, bypass the conventional restaurants and step into a *salumeria* or *rosticceria,* which are fancy delicatessens with wonderful assortments and varieties, albeit served on paper plates.

- *Pizzas* exist in Italy, but they are usually individual with thin, crispy crusts.

- Strong regional traits exist, especially in the spoken language. Northern Italians look down their noses at southerners, and vice versa, and neither say they can understand residents of Sardinia. But don't let this deter you from trying your school Italian — it will be understood and greeted warmly wherever you go.

- Shaking hands is done much more frequently than in the United States. It is done every time when meeting and when leaving.

- The Italian for *Mr., Mrs.,* and *Miss* and the rules for their use differ somewhat from other languages. A woman is addressed as *Signora,* whether she is married or not. A girl is addressed as *Signorina.* But the term *Signore* is used only with the other person's surname; it is used alone only by service people — waiters or shop assistants — and is comparable to *Sir.*

- A university degree qualifies Italians to be called by professional titles. Not only are male doctors called *dottore,* but engineers are called *ingegnere,* teachers at any level are called *professore,* and accountants are called *ragioniere.* The same is true for women, except the feminine versions are used (that is, *dottoressa, professoressa,* etc.)

- Pronunciation in Italian is fairly easy to learn, and once learned, you will be able to pronounce most Italian words.


Here is your handy guide to key Italian words and phrases:

| | |
|---|---|
| please | *pehr fah-VOH-ray* |
| | or *pehr peeah-CHEE-ray* |
| thank you | *GRAH-tseeay* |

| good morning/ afternoon | *bwohn JOR-noh* |
| good evening | *bwoh-na SAY-rah* |
| Where is . . .? | *Doh-VEH eel . . .?* |
| bathroom | *gah-bee-NAYT-toh* |
| hotel | *oh-TELL* |
| yes | *see* |
| no | *noh* |
| excuse me | *mee SKOO-zee* |
| pleased to meet you | *peeah-CHA Y-ray* |
| Help! | Aay-UTT-oh |

## SPANISH

In the United States today, it is quite easy—almost expected—to hear Spanish spoken around us. Spanish-speaking radio and TV programs issue from every large city, tides of migrant workers flow into the northern states each summer, and our schools have a long history of teaching Spanish.

Some twenty-five million Hispanics now live in the United States, and with the advent of the North American Free Trade Agreement, the Spanish language will become even more pervasive. In fact, Spanish has become so widespread in the United States that, in protest, several states have considered passing legislation to make English the official language.

For a country that is already considered monolingual, this is unfortunate. Spanish is a lovely language, not difficult to learn in comparison to many others; and once learned, it allows one to automatically comprehend portions of Italian, Portuguese (especially in the written form), and some French, because all are so-called romance languages with strong Latin roots. For Americans wishing to learn Spanish, pronunciation is relatively easy. This is because in Spanish the five vowels and most consonants are pronounced exactly the same way each and every time.

For the Hispanics, it's the other way around. Pronunciation is the biggest bugaboo when striving to learn American English. Our spelling and pronunciation are inconsistent and frustrating.

Because pronunciation in Spanish is so consistent, most Latins can look at and pronounce any Spanish word, whether or not they have ever heard it before or know its meaning. In fact, it is said that few (if any) spelling bees are conducted in Latin countries, because Spanish spelling and pronunciation march in step alongside each other. An educated Latin never makes spelling errors, whereas an American with a Ph.D. can easily misspell English words.

To appreciate what Spanish-speaking people (and others) go through when trying to learn the mysteries of pronunciation and spelling in American English, consider this little ditty:

Beware of *heard*, a dreadful word
That looks like *beard* but sounds like *bird*,
And *dead*: it's said like *bed*, not *bead*,
For goodness sake don't call it *deed*!
Watch out for *meat* and *great* and *threat*
(They rhyme with *suite* and *straight* and *debt*).
A *moth* is not a *moth* as in *mother*
Nor *both* in *bother*, nor *broth* in *brother*,
And *here* is not a match for *there*,
Nor *dear* and *fear*, for *bear* and *pear*.

What should you do when traveling in Spanish-speaking lands? Here are two important answers from Professor Lucia Caycedos Garner from Bogota, Colombia, who teaches in the Department of Spanish and Portuguese at the University of Wisconsin. First, she advises that there is something more important than just learning the basic phrases of a language. That is learning some fundamentals about the culture of a country before you visit it. People can be very forgiving about hearing mistakes in their language if their culture is respected. This is especially true in the diverse countries that comprise Latin America.

Second, Professor Garner urges Americans to slow down their speech and avoid mumbling. Latin listeners have great difficulty comprehending American English when it is spoken rapidly.

Here are general pieces of advice when traveling anywhere in Central or South America:

- The Spanish spoken in, say, Argentina is different from that heard in, say, Mexico. There are differences in words, terms, and pronunciation. This explains why Latins from, say, Ecuador can usually identify Latins from, say, Chile by their speech; this holds true throughout the whole region.

- Aside from language, there are other cultural differences between the many countries scattered throughout Latin America. Consequently, each has a healthy amount of national pride. To dramatize this fact, two Central American countries once actually went to war simply over the outcome of a soccer match between the two.

- Heed Professor Garner's advice and take care to learn as much as possible about the cultural background of any Latin country that you visit.

- Cuban Spanish is probably the most difficult to comprehend because Cubans tend to drop letters and syllables and also because they seem to string words together.

- Conversely, the Spanish used in countries like Colombia is considered "purer," with more distinct pronunciation, and, therefore, it is easier for students of Spanish to comprehend.

- When conversing throughout Latin America, be sure to use and respect titles. As is the custom in other parts of the world, use *Senor* ("Mr."), *Senorita* ("Miss"), and *Senora* ("Mrs.") until invited to use first names. Be equally respectful of titles like *Doctor* and *Professor*.

- Adult men and women add their mother's family name to theirs. As a result, the name *Luis Alvarez Montoya* signifies the following: *Luis* is the given name, *Alvarez* is the father's family name, and *Montoya* is the mother's maiden name. Therefore, this man is called *Señor Alvarez*, but since there may be many, many Alvarez families, you know that he comes from the Alvarez family whose matriarch was originally a Montoya.

- Occasionally, you will hear a respected, elderly gentleman given the title of *Don*. This is merely an extra title of respect and is flattering to the recipient.

- Bear in mind that Brazil was colonized by the Portuguese; therefore, the national language there is Portuguese.

- Hispanics now represent the second largest minority group in the United States, numbering almost 25 million, or 10 percent of our population. Moreover, Hispanics are the fastest-growing minority in the United States. Also, approximately half of that number trace their origins to Mexico.

- Puerto Rico is a U.S. possession and enjoys commonwealth status within the United States. This means its residents are citizens of the United States. Its population of about 3.5 million learn English as a second language, so American English is widely understood there.

- Special tips for our closest Spanish-speaking neighbor, Mexico, include:

  — Mexicans like wordplay, quotations, and (what seems to Americans like) flowery language.

  — An American says, "I am delighted to meet you." A Mexican says (in Spanish), "I am enchanted to meet you." As author John C. Condon explains, "The distance between these words is a good measure of the distance between the two cultural styles, a distance which is but a small step for the Mexican but an awkward leap for many Americans."

  — In Mexico, lawyers are respectfully referred to as *licenciado* (with their family name following).

  — Remember that Mexico is in America too. Also, the correct name for that country is the United States of Mexico.

(Note: For two insightful books on the Mexican culture, obtain John C. Condon's *Good Neighbors, Communicating with the Mexicans*, (Intercultural Press, 1985) and *The Mexicans, An Inside View of a Changing Society*, by Paula Heusinkveld (John Wiley & Sons, 1994).

Helpful words and phrases that you might memorize are as follows:

| | |
|---|---|
| please | *por-fah-VOHR* |
| thank you | *GRA-see-ahs* |
| good morning/ good day | *bwayn-oss DEE-ahs* |
| good afternoon | *bwayn-ahs TAR-days* |
| good evening | *bwayn-ahs NHO-chess* |
| Where is . . .? | *DOHN-day ehsta . . .?* |
| bathroom | *BAHN-yo* |
| hotel | *oh-TELL* |
| yes | *SEE* |
| no | *NOH* |
| Help! | *So-KHOR-oh!* |
| very good/well | *mwee BWAYN-oh/bee-YEN* |

## CHINESE

Unless you plan to be a serious student of Chinese and devote months and years to its study, probably the best you can hope for, in being able to communicate with the Chinese, is memorizing a few words and phrases. Otherwise, as a businessperson or as a tourist, communicating is best left to an interpreter.

There are several reasons for this:

1. China is a vast country with dozens of different dialects, which are as different as French is from Spanish or English is from German.

2. Chinese is a tone language, which means that the *pitch* of a syllable helps determine meaning. The same word, said with different tones, can mean entirely different things. This is normally difficult for Americans to learn.

3. There are other differences between Chinese and American English that complicate comprehension. For example, verbs in Chinese don't change tenses; subjects and objects can be the same word; and nouns do not have a gender, so mistakes such as *his husband* or *her wife* occur frequently.

4. There is absolutely no relationship between written Chinese and written English. Chinese consists of over 230,000 characters, or symbols. The average Chinese knows about 4,000 to 6,000 of these through memorization.

In spite of all this, in 1993, more than 332,000 Americans were expected to visit China. And with that figure on the rise, serious attempts to communicate should be made by both sides.

From the Chinese side, American English is especially difficult. According to Clara Shu-Yi Sun, who was born and raised in Beijing, China, and is a lecturer in East Asian languages and literature at the University of Wisconsin, the Chinese find our grammar, slang, and pronunciation extremely difficult.

Still, the two cultures must cope, and here are some insights that might help:

- Loan words can be dangerous. Here are some examples:

  — Americans use the word *kowtow* to mean to defer, or to be subservient to another person. But the meaning in Chinese is literally to kneel and touch one's forehead to the ground.

  — When we say someone was *shanghaied,* we mean someone was captured or tricked into some type of situation. But in Chinese, *Shanghai* is not only a prominent city but also a word meaning "to exhort."

  — We talk about being *gung ho,* meaning enthusiastic, but in Chinese, it simply means "together" and "a republic."

- A system was devised and adopted in 1979 to standardize the spelling of Chinese words into Western languages. It is called the Pinyin system. For example, prior to 1979, the name of the capital city of China was Peking, but since it was pronounced more like *Beijing*, it was converted to that spelling.

- The simple words *yes* and *no* are not used in Chinese. Instead, the verb being used is either affirmed or negated.

- Written Chinese—which consists of pictographs rather than words as we know them—is universally known and recognized throughout the nation; spoken Chinese, however, is divided into so many different dialects that the Chinese people have great difficulty understanding one another unless something is in writing.

- Mandarin is the most popular Chinese dialect and is spoken in the Beijing region, which is also the seat of government; Shanghainese is, obviously, spoken in the Shanghai region on the west coast; and Cantonese is spoken in the south, in the cities of Canton (now called Guangzhou) and Hong Kong. In the Republic of China (Taiwan), Mandarin is the official and most common dialect.

- One reason why the pronunciation of American English is strange for Chinese is because there is no hard *r* sound in their language. (Try speaking English and omitting the *r* sound.)

- Here are examples of how tones and pronunciation affect Chinese words:

    — If you say the word *tang* in a level, relatively high tone, it means "soup"; if you say it with a rising inflection, it means "sugar."

    — If you say the word *gou* with a falling-then-rising inflection, it means "dog"; if you say it with a falling inflection only, it means "enough."

Completely separate from these differences between Chinese and American English are differences in our *style* of communication. Here are some examples:

1. American communication can be likened to an arrow. Asians, on the other hand, are taught to be indirect, mainly to avoid any possibility of offending the other person or hurting his or her feelings. Therefore, the American inclination for directness or candor is considered rude among the Chinese.

2. Also, showing impatience, anxiety, or anger is considered "immature, unprofessional, boorish or untrustworthy," according to author Angi Ma Wong.

3. Body language is also interpreted differently. Direct eye contact, standing with your hands in your pockets, pointing with your index finger, touching—all are considered impolite among the Chinese.

4. Modesty plays an important part in mannerisms, speech, dress, and general communication style.

5. What Americans would label as *superstition* is integrated into Chinese life and is embodied in the term *feng shui*. The words *feng shui* mean "the wind and the water," and the term represents the power of the natural environment. Throughout China, *feng shui* masters are relied upon to divine the future for good or ill fortune, especially in relation to locations. For that reason, many Chinese will not construct a building without consulting a *feng shui* expert.

6. Similarly, certain colors and numbers carry special meanings.

   - The number eight is considered the luckiest number because it sounds like a word that means "to prosper."

   - Four is an unlucky number because it sounds like the word for "death" or "to die."

   - The color red symbolizes joy and happiness.

   - Green means health, growth, family life, youth, and prosperity.

- White is the funeral color because it is connected with re-birth and purity, and black is linked with guilt, evil, death and mourning (as in the West).

Finally, the best piece of advice for communicating with the Chinese can be encapsuled in just two words: *patience* and *politeness*. Carry plentiful supplies of both with you.

Here are a few words and phrases (in Mandarin) that might help smooth your path when dealing with the Chinese:

| please | *ching* |
| thank you | *she-YEH she-yeh* |
| good morning | *dzow-AN* |
| good afternoon | *she-ah-woo HOW* |
| good evening | *wan AN* |
| good night | *wan AN* |
| Where is . . .? | *. . . dzy NARR* |
| bathroom | *tsuhe-swore* |
| yes | *shi* (the closest to *yes*) |
| no | *BOO* (the closest to *no*) |
| Help! | *Jee-yoh ming!* |
| very good/well | *hun how* |

For a helpful book on communicating with Orientals, read *TARGET, The U.S. Asian Market, A Practical Guide to Doing Business*, by Angi Ma Wong, Pacific Heritage Books, P.O. Box 3967-BB, Palos Verdes, CA 90274-9547.

# Glossaries

## AUSTRALIAN ENGLISH TO AMERICAN ENGLISH

Note: The following list is reproduced with the kind permission of the Australian Tourist Commission, 489 Fifth Avenue, 31st Floor, New York, NY 10017; Telephone: (212) 687-6300. Some of these words, like *bloke, barmy,* and *cuppa,* are also used and known in the United Kingdom.

**Alice, The**   The city of Alice Springs, in the Northern territory.

**amber fluid**   Beer. As in "Let's have a quick transfusion of amber fluid."

**ankle-biter**   A small child. See "rug-rat."

**ANZAC**   Members of the Australian and New Zealand Army Corps in World War I. Anzac Day, which falls on April 25, is a national holiday. Also, delicious biscuits (cookies), made with oats and golden syrup are known as Anzacs.

**apples**   Everything's under control, as in "She's apples."

**Apple Isle, The**   Tasmania, Australia's only island state.

**arvo**   Afternoon. "Pop in for arvo tea."

**Aussie salute**   The back and forth waving of hands before the face to shoo away the flies. See "blowie.

**back of beyond**   Way out there somewhere; remote.

**bag of fruit**   Rhyming slang for a man's suit. As in "He was dressed to kill in his bag of fruit and he didn't care who knew it."

**Balmain bug**   Small type of crayfish. Named after the trawlermen of the historic Sydney suburb of Balmain who pioneered the industry.

**barbie**   Barbecue. "Let's go down to the beach and have a barbie." Also, "He's a few snags (sausages) short of a barbie" is used to describe someone who is a little crazy.

**barney**   An argument or a dispute.

**barrack**   To give encouragement to your sports team.

**barramundi**   Aboriginal name for a large tasty fish found in the waters of Queensland, Northern Territory, and Western Australia.

**bastard**   A term of abuse, but it can also be one of male endearment, as in, "G'day ya silly old bastard." Warning: use it in a jocular way or you may get into a blue.

**battler**   Someone who struggles hard to make ends meet. "He's a real Aussie battler."

**beaut or beauty**   Great! Terrific! Also pronounced "beaudy," or "bewdy."

**big-note**   To boast and exaggerate one's wealth and power.

**billabong**   A water hole in a dry river bed. "Once a jolly swagman camped by a billabong . . ."

**billy**   A metal can, usually tin, enamel ware, or aluminum used for making tea over an open fire.

**black stump**   An imaginary point dividing civilization and the Outback. "She's the biggest big-noter this side of the black stump."

**bloke**   A male; the guy in charge.

**bloody**   One of the most overused adjectives in the Australian vocabulary, bloody is used to add emphasis to almost any expression, as in "She's a bloody beauty," [or] "Too bloody right, mate."

**blowie**   A blowfly. Sometimes jokingly referred to as Australia's national bird. See "Aussie salute."

**bludger**  Someone who doesn't pull [his or her] weight at work and sponges on others.

**blue**  To have an argument or a fight.

**blue heeler**  A nuggety cattle dog with a blue-flecked coat, popular with bushies and city folk alike.

**Bluey**  Nickname for a bloke with red hair. Also, a "swagman's" (tramp's) blanket roll.

**bonzer**  Someone (or something) who performs well. As in "He's a bonzer bloke to have on your side in a blue."

**boomer**  A large male kangaroo. It is believed by some Aussie youngsters that Santa Claus's sleigh is pulled by six white "boomers."

**boot**  The trunk of a car.

**bottler**  Someone (or something) who performs well. "He's a little bottler."

**bottle shop**  A liquor store, often part of a hotel.

**brolly**  An umbrella.

**brumby**  From an Aboriginal word meaning a wild horse.

**bubbler**  A drinking fountain.

**bucket, to**  To dump on someone; to blame [one] for everything.

**Buckley's chance**  Absolutely no chance. As in "She's got two chances: Buckley's and none."

**bull artist**  A teller of tall tales; a braggart. Closely-related to a "big-noter."

**Bundy**  The town of Bundaberg in Queensland. Also the name of a popular brand of rum.

**bung, to**  To put on an act; to throw. As in "There's no need to bung it on with me." Also, "Just bung another prawn (shrimp) on the barbie."

**Bush, The**  Unspoiled land beyond the city with natural vegetation. Also, "to go bush" is to get away from all your troubles. As in "Bruce's gone bush."

**bushie**  Used to describe someone who lives miles from anywhere. "Bazza's a real bushie."

**bushranger**  An outlaw in early colonial days. Ned Kelly was one of Australia's most notorious bushrangers.

**bush tucker**  Native food such as berries, roots, and foodstuffs, such as edible insects, known to the Aborigines and only recently discovered by European Australians.

**B.Y.O.**  "Bring your own." Unlicensed restaurant where you need to bring your own alcohol. Also, many party invitations include the B.Y.O. proviso.

**Captain Cook**  British navigator and explorer who mapped the east coast of Australia in 1776. Also, "take a Captain Cook" is rhyming slang for take a look.

**cheese and kisses**  Rhyming slang for wife, i.e. "the missus."

**chemist**  A pharmacy or drugstore

**china**  Rhyming slang for mate. "Me ole china plate."

**chips**  French fries or potato crisps. To "spit chips" means that you are very angry.

**chook**  Domestic chicken or hen. Some Australians keep chooks in the back garden (yard) in a chook house with a chook run. "He's running around like a headless chook" refers to someone who is overexcited or disorganized.

**Chrissie**  Christmas; Chrissie prezzie (present).

**Clayton's**  Name of a soft drink that was promoted as a substitute for alcohol. The term came to mean something that is not what it seems. "This is a bloody Clayton's dictionary if ever I saw one."

**Coathanger, The**  Term for the Sydney Harbor Bridge.

**cobber**  A close friend.

**cocky**  A cockatoo, native bird of Australia. Can also mean a farmer; Boss Cocky means the boss; and someone who is cocky is overconfident.

**cooee**  Originally a call used by Aborigines in the bush, it is now used by all Australians. To be "within cooee" is to be in earshot.

**cop, to**  Take a look at that! "Cop that." Also, "Cop it sweet" means to be fortunate.

**Corroboree**  Aboriginal dance ceremony or meeting.

**crook** To be sick or no good; also angry. "Don't go crook on me for getting crook."

**crows, stone the** A mild oath.

**cruel, to** A ruined opportunity. "He cruelled his chances by getting crook."

**cuppa** A cup of tea. "What you need is a good cuppa." The Australian antidote to all problems.

**dag** Basically a nerd or even a little worse.

**damper** Traditionally, unleavened bread baked in the ashes of a fire. The name comes from the practice of damping the fire so the bread can be cooked in the glowing embers.

**dead-set** Absolute; genuine. "He's a dead-set mate," or "Is that dead-set?"

**digger** Originally a miner in the goldfields, now used to refer to an Australian soldier.

**dill** A simpleton or a fool.

**dilly-bag** A small woven bag carried by Aboriginal women. Often used to describe a small bag of any sort.

**dingo** A native dog.

**dobber** An informant who has "dobbed in" someone. "A bloke wouldn't dob in a mate."

**Dover** The brand name of a bushman's knife. "To flash one's Dover" means to open a clasp knife to begin a meal.

**drongo** A real fool or a moron.

**dummy, spit the** To lose one's temper.

**dumper** The bane of all surfers, a dumper is a large wave that tosses you around like a piece of driftwood instead of carrying you in to shore.

**dunny** Originally an unsewered toilet at the bottom of the garden (yard), now used generally for the toilet.

**earbasher** Someone who talks endlessly; a bore.

**Esky** Brand name but now used generically for a cooler to carry drinks and food to barbies and parties.

**fair dinkum**   True, genuine; an assertion of truth or genuineness. "It's true, mate, fair dinkum."

**fair go**   A chance, an equal opportunity. "Give us a fair go, Bruce."

**fang**   To drive around at high speed. "Let's fang up to the beach."

**first cab off the rank**   To jump at an opportunity; quick off the mark.

**flat out**   Very busy. "He's flat out like a lizard drinking."

**floater**   A meat pie in a plate of soupy peas or gravy.

**footy**   Refers to either Rugby League, Rugby Union, or Australian Rules football, which is very popular in Melbourne.

**fossick**   Originally meant to search or pick around for gold or gemstones, but is now used in the more general sense of searching for something.

**Fremantle doctor**   Cool breeze that blows in off the Indian Ocean during the hot summer months of December to March.

**furphy**   Originally the brand name of a water-cart but now means a rumor or phony story.

**galah**   Native bird with a grey back and pink front. Also, a fool. "You're a bit of a galah."

**garbo**   Garbage man.

**give it a burl**   Give it a go.

**googie**   An egg. To be "full as a goog" is to be drunk.

**grasshopper**   A bush term for a tourist, especially in tourist groups: "They eat everthing in sight and never have a drink." Also known as grassie.

**greenie**   A mildly derogatory term for a conservationist.

**grey ghost**   Parking police in New South Wales (because of the color of their uniforms).

**grog**   General name for all alcohol. A "grog-on" or "grog-up" is a drinking party.

**grouse**   Very good. "That's a grouse pie floater."

**gum tree**   Eucalyptus tree. There are many different types of gum trees. To be "up a gum tree" means you are in trouble.

**hard yakka**   Hard work.

**heaps, to give**  To give someone a hard time.

**heart starter**  The first alcoholic drink of the day.

**hoon**  A lout. Also, to hoon around.

**hooray**  Goodbye, so long. Also, Hooroo!

**jackeroo**  A young male ranch hand.

**jillaroo**  A young female ranch hand.

**joey**  Baby kangaroo or wallaby.

**jumbuck**  A sheep. A jumbuck barber is a sheepshearer.

**jumper**  A sweater.

**kanga**  Kangaroo. In the bush, to "have a bit of kanga" is to have some cash. Kanga cricket is a form of the game designed for children.

**kelpie**  An Australian breed of short-haired dog, used to herd sheep.

**koala**  A lovable nocturnal marsupial, often mistakenly referred to as a bear. It is found only in Australia where it spends much of its time eating a special type of gum leaf and dozing on a tree branch.

**kookaburra**  Australian kingfisher bird with brown and white feathers and a distinctive, almost human laugh.

**kylie**  The West Australian Nyungar Aboriginal word for boomerang.

**lair**  A show-off. "Mug lair" is an abusive term for someone who is both stupid and vulgar. "That bloke's a mug lair mongrel."

**larrikin**  An urban hooligan with a dash of style.

**lash out, to**  Spend money freely. Also, "lashings," which means lots of something—especially food and drink.

**legless**  Someone who is so drunk they can't walk.

**lolly**  Candy or boiled sweet. Lolly water is a soft drink. Also, "to do your lolly" is to lose your temper.

**loo**  The toilet or bathroom.

**lurk, to**  To act suspiciously. Also, a "lurk merchant" is someone who is a shrewd operator.

**mate**  Friend, buddy. The great Australian leveller. Anyone can be your mate, from the prime minister to the bloke next door.

**Matilda**  A swag or bedroll. To waltz Matilda is to carry a swag.

**mental, to chuck a**   To lose one's temper. "Kylie really chucked a mental at the barbie last night."

**middy**   A medium-sized (9 oz.) glass of beer.

**moral**   A sure thing. "A moral certainty."

**mozzie**   A mosquito.

**muddie**   Mud crab. Large delicious crab found in the mangrove wetlands of Queensland and New South Wales.

**mullet, stunned**   Someone who is dazed or uncomprehending. "Hey mate, you looked like a bloody stunned mullet."

**nana, to be off one's**   To be mentally deranged or to lose your temper. "He was off his nana."

**nipper**   A small child.

**Noah's Ark**   Rhyming slang for a shark.

**no-hoper**   A fool, or lazy, hapless person.

**nong**   A fool or silly person.

**ocker**   An uncultivated Australian. Easily identified by [his or her] navy cotton singlet (undershirt) or T-shirt, short shorts, and thongs. Used in the same way as "redneck" in the U.S.

**off**   Many meanings, such as tainted food is "off"; bad taste is also "off"; to leave in a hurry is to be "off"; and if someone is ill they are "feeling off."

**old man**   A fully grown male kangaroo.

**paralytic**   Dead drunk.

**pavlova**   A popular suburban dessert.

**pie floater**   Meat pie floating in a bowl of pea soup.

**pokies**   Poker or slot machines.

**pollie**   Politician. Australians, like many people, don't hold "bloody pollies" in high regard.

**pommy**   Someone from the British Isles. Several explanations: pomegranate for [the] ruddy red cheeks of British immigrants; [or because] the acronym P.O.M.E. stamped on early convicts' clothing stood for Prisoner of Mother England.

**possie**   A position or spot. "There's a good parking possie."

**P-plate**  Provisional-plate. Newly licensed drivers in Australia have to display a P-plate for one year and are known as P-platers.

**prang**  A car crash or accident.

**prawn**  What Americans call a shrimp. Also, a fool. "Don't come the raw prawn with me, mate" means don't try and pull a fast one.

**pull your head in**  Mind your own business.

**Rafferty's rules**  No rules at all.

**rager**  Someone who likes to party.

**ratbag**  A bit of a rogue or troublemaker.

**ratty**  Mad or deranged.

**razoo**  An imaginary coin of no value. Also, to have no money. "She doesn't have a brass razoo."

**reggo**  Motor vehicle registration.

**ring-in**  Something replaced fraudulently. Like the American word "ringer."

**ripper**  Someone or something really good. "Bloody ripper, mate."

**ropeable**  Angry or bad tempered.

**rort**  A fraudulent act. Aussies are always accusing the pollies of rorting the system.

**roughie**  A cheat, someone who tries to "pull a swifties." Also refers to someone who is uncouth.

**round**  Originally, to round up cattle, but nowadays refers to buying a "round" of drinks at the pub. (And it's rude to miss your turn at buying.)

**rug-rat**  A small child. See "ankle-biter."

**sanger**  A sandwich. Also "sango."

**shag on a rock**  Being exposed or alone. "Left like a shag on a rock."

**shandy**  A drink composed mostly of beer [with] a dash of lemonade. Once regarded as a "refined" drink for ladies, [it is] now popular primarily with older women.

**sheila**  A young girl or woman. Less popular today in light of feminism.

**sherbert**  A beer. "There's nothing better after a day at the beach than a few sherberts."

**shout, to**  To pay for a round of drinks. "It's your shout, mate."

**silvertail**  Someone with social aspirations; can also refer to a wealthy person.

**singlet**  Mostly worn by men under their shirts; a sleeveless T-shirt.

**skerrick**  A small amount.

**skite, to**  To boast or to brag.

**sling-off, to**  To ridicule or mock.

**snag**  A light meal, but most commonly a sausage.

**snaky**  Angry. "Listen you drongo. Don't get snaky with me." Can also mean sneaky.

**sook**  A coward or sissy.

**sparrow fart**  Very early in the morning.

**spine-bash, to**  To loaf or lie around.

**sport**  A friendly greeting, as in "G'day sport."

**station**  A ranch where cattle or sheep are the major industry.

**sticky beak**  A nosy, prying person.

**stir, to**  To provoke someone. A stirrer is a troublemaker.

**strides**  Men's trousers.

**sundowner**  Itinerant worker. Originally a tramp who wandered from station to station looking for work, making sure he arrived at sundown in time for dinner.

**swagman**  A tramp; an itinerant worker. Also known as a swaggie.

**swimmers**  Bathing suit.

**ta**  Thank you. "Ta ta" means good-bye, and to go "ta tas" means to go on an outing.

**Tassie**  Tasmania.

**Taswegian**  Tasmanian.

**tinnie**  A can of beer.

**togs**  Bathing suit.

**too right!**  Certainly!

**toot**  The toilet.

**troppo**  To "go troppo" is to be mentally disturbed.

**tube**  Can of beer.

**tucker**  To eat food.

**turps**  Alcoholic liquor. "Let's have a night on the turps."

**two-bob**  Cheap; of little value. Also, "as mad as a two-bob watch" means silly or mad.

**up a gum tree**  Confused, not sure what to do.

**ute**  A utility truck or pick-up truck.

**Vegemite**  Loved by all true-blue Aussies, Vegemite is a brown yeast extract spread on toast and sandwiches. Sometimes referred to as Australia's national food.

**waddy waddy**  Dried beef similar to, but much harder than, beef jerky.

**walkabout, to**  To wander the countryside.

**Waltzing Matilda**  Australia's unofficial national anthem. Also means to wander around the country with a swag (bedroll).

**Westralian**  Someone from Western Australia.

**whacker**  A fool. A general term of abuse.

**whacko**  A positive exclamation, such as in "That sheila Shirl is a fair dinkum, beauty bottler, whacko the chook little Aussie battler, if I ever laid eyes on one."

**whinge, to**  To complain a lot. A whinger is a person who whinges.

**woomera**  An Aboriginal implement used to propel a spear.

**wowser**  Someone whose behavior is puritanical or prudish.

**yakka**  Hard work. "She's a demon for hard yakka."

**yobbo**  A hoodlum.

# AMERICAN ENGLISH TO ENGLISH ENGLISH

Note: This glossary was compiled by John McGill, now a retired executive of the 3M Corporation. John and his wife took under their wing many Americans who were transferred to England by 3M. The first requirement was always a basic glossary such as this. My thanks to the McGills for allowing me to reproduce it here.

| American | English |
|---|---|
| apartment house | block of flats |
| baby carriage | pram (short for perambulator) |
| backside | bottom, or buttocks |
| baggage checkroom | left luggage |
| ballpoint pen | biro, or ballpoint |
| Band-Aids | sticking plaster, or elastoplast |
| barber | gentleman's hairdresser |
| base plug | power point |
| bathroom | WC (water closet) |
| beauty parlor | ladies hairdresser |
| billboard | hoarding |
| bobby pin | kirby grip |
| broil | grill |
| burlap | hessian |
| can | tin |
| candy | sweets |
| candy store | sweetshop |
| check (from a bank) | cheque |
| checkers (the game) | draughts |
| chicory | endive |
| chips (potato) | crisps |
| cleaning woman | daily help, or a char |
| closet | cupboard, or wardrobe |
| coat | jacket |
| confectioner's sugar | icing sugar |
| cookies | sweet biscuits |
| corner (of a street) | turning |
| cornmeal | sometimes called Polenta |
| cornstarch | cornflour |

| | |
|---|---|
| cotton | cotton wool |
| cracker | biscuit, or a toy that "pops" when a tab is pulled |
| crib | cot |
| cuffs (on pants) | turn-ups (on trousers) |
| curb | kerb |
| dead-end street | cul-de-sac |
| dessert | sweet, pudding, or dessert |
| detour | diversion |
| diapers | nappies |
| dish towel | tea towel |
| divided highway | dual carriageway |
| do the dishes | wash up |
| drugstore | chemist |
| eggplant | aubergine |
| electric cord | flex |
| elevator | lift |
| endive | chicory |
| eraser | rubber |
| faucet | tap |
| fender | wing |
| first floor | ground floor |
| fix | repair, or mend |
| flashlight | torch |
| flat (tire) | puncture (tyre) |
| french fries | chips |
| furnace | boiler |
| garbage dump | rubbish tip |
| garbage pail | pedal bin, or rubbish bin |
| garden | vegetable patch |
| garters | suspenders |
| gas or gasoline | petrol (except in cooking) |
| gear shift (car) | gear lever |
| generator (car) | dynamo, or alternator |
| gingersnaps | ginger nuts |
| girdle (lightweight) | roll-on |
| glasses (for the eyes) | spectacles, or glasses |
| graham crackers | digestive biscuits |

| | |
|---|---|
| homework | prep |
| hood (car) | bonnet |
| install | fix |
| installment plan | hire purchase |
| intermission (of a play) | interval |
| jail | gaol (same pronunciation) |
| Jell-O | jelly |
| jelly | jam, or preserves |
| kerosene | paraffin |
| lawyer | solicitor (notary), barrister (advocate), or lawyer (either) |
| lettuce, iceberg | web lettuce |
| lettuce, romaine | cos lettuce |
| lima beans | rare in England, but young broad beans are close |
| mail | post mail box, post box, or pillar box |
| molasses | treacle |
| movie | cine film, or just film |
| movies, movie theater | cinema |
| muffler (car) | silencer |
| muslin | calico |
| nauseated | sick |
| notions | haberdashery |
| orchestra seats | stalls |
| pants | trousers |
| panty hose | tights |
| parking brake | hand brake |
| parking lights | side lights |
| pitcher | jug |
| pot holder | oven glove, or kettle holder |
| presently | now |
| private room in a hospital | private ward |

| | |
|---|---|
| purse or pocketbook | handbag or bag (a purse is small, just for coins; a wallet is for folding money) |
| realtor | estate agent |
| reserve (a table) | book |
| round-trip (ticket) | return |
| rubber boots | wellies, or wellington boots |
| rubbing alcohol | surgical spirits |
| run (in a stocking) | ladder |
| salesclerk | shop (or sales) assistant |
| saltines | water biscuits |
| sanitary napkins | sanitary towels |
| scallions | spring onions |
| second floor | first floor |
| sedan (car) | saloon (car) |
| sheer muslin | muslin |
| shrimp | shrimp come in 3 sizes: small ones are *shrimp*; medium ones *prawns*; and large ones *scampi*. |
| sick (with a cold) | ill |
| sidewalk | pavement or footpath |
| slipcovers | loose covers |
| snaps | press studs, or poppers |
| sneakers | plimsolls, tennis shoes, gym shoes, or trainers |
| soon | soon or presently |
| specialist (medical) | consultant or specialist (with Mr. instead of Dr. preceding name) |
| spool of thread | reel of cotton |
| stand in line | to queue (pronounced *cue*) |
| stove | cooker (a stove is an old-style room heater) |
| subway | underground, or tube (a subway is a pedestrian tunnel) |
| sunsquash | marrow |
| suspenders | braces |
| sweater | jumper, jersey, or sweater |

| | |
|---|---|
| telephone, to | ring up, to |
| thumbtack | drawing pin |
| topcoat | overcoat |
| trash can, garbage can | dustbin |
| truck | van (panel truck), lorry (large truck), or truck |
| trunk (car) | boot |
| underpants (women) | panties, knickers, or briefs |
| undershirt | vest |
| undershorts (men) | pants |
| unlisted telephone | ex-directory |
| vacation | holiday |
| vest | waistcoat |
| wash up | wash one's hands, or go to the bathroom |
| windshield | windscreen |
| wrench | spanner (a wrench is a large plumber's spanner) |
| yard | garden (a yard is a small paved area behind the house) |
| yellow turnip (rutabaga) | swede |
| zipper | zip |
| zucchini | courgette |

## NEW ZEALAND ENGLISH TO AMERICAN ENGLISH

| *New Zealand* | *American* |
|---|---|
| aided school | one originally founded by the church |
| arterial road | major road, or trunk road |
| articulated lorry | trailer truck |
| assistant | salesclerk in a store |
| autumn | fall |
| bank holiday | legal holiday |
| barman/barmaid | bartender |

| | |
|---|---|
| barrister | trial lawyer |
| bed-board | headboard |
| beetroot | beet |
| bend (in a road) | curve |
| block of ice | ice cube |
| Boxing Day | the day after Christmas when gifts are left for service people (e.g., mail carrier, garbage collector) |
| brassed off | angry |
| bread bin | bread box |
| call box | outside public telephone |
| caravan | house trailer |
| caretaker | janitor, or building superintendent |
| car park | parking lot |
| casket | jewel box; coffin |
| castor sugar | finely granulated sugar |
| change down | downshift in car gears |
| chap | guy, or fellow |
| cheap | reduced in price |
| cheeky | rude, or naughty |
| chilly bin | cooler for picnics |
| commercial traveller | salesperson |
| company | corporation |
| conkers | children's game |
| cooker | stove |
| corporation | city or municipal government |
| county borough | county seat |
| crib | vacation flat (on South Island) |
| cupboard | closet |
| daft | strange |
| dairy | convenience store |
| davenport | writing table |
| dear | expensive |
| decorate | paint |
| digs | rooms, or lodging |

| director (of a company) | officer |
| dispenser | pharmacist |
| double-glazed | storm windows |
| dustbin | garbage or trash can |
| early closing | when shops close early on one day of the week |
| enquiries | information |
| fag | cigarette |
| fanny | vagina |
| Father Christmas | Santa Claus |
| fender | bumper |
| first floor | second floor |
| flannel | washcloth |
| flex | electric cord |
| fridge | refrigerator |
| full stop | a period in punctuation |
| Girl Guide | Girl Scout |
| giveway | yield (as in traffic) |
| grammar school | college preparatory school for ages 11–19 |
| grease-proof paper | wax paper |
| guillotine | paper cutter |
| gum boots | high rubber boots |
| head boy/girl | top boy/girl in school |
| headmaster | principal of a school |
| inverted commas | quotation marks |
| jacket potato | baked potato |
| jack up | to arrange or organize |
| joiner | carpenter |
| kindie | preschool for ages 3–5 |
| larder | pantry |
| lay-by | rest area on a highway; putting a deposit on a purchase and paying in installments |
| lay on | to provide or arrange for |
| leaver (school) | graduating student |

| | |
|---|---|
| lemonade | comparable to Seven Up; not a lemon drink |
| M.P. | Member of Parliament |
| match | game |
| mend | to repair |
| milk float | milk truck |
| mind | to watch out for |
| mineral | soft drink |
| motor coach | bus |
| newsagent | news/magazine dealer or store |
| notice board | bulletin board |
| old boy/girl | alumnus/alumna |
| on the dole | unemployed and on welfare |
| panel beater | auto body shop |
| Pavlova | famous New Zealand dessert |
| personal call | person-to-person telephone call |
| pitch | field for playing cricket |
| reception | front office or desk |
| resident | a person registered at a hotel |
| ring binder | loose-leaf notebook |
| rubber | eraser |
| schools: | |
|    kindie/kindergarten | for ages 3–5 |
|    primary school | for ages 5–10 |
|    intermediate school | for ages 11–12 |
|    secondary school | for ages 13–17 |
|    university | for ages 17 and over |
| school term | school semester |
| shout | to buy a round of drinks |
| smashing | terrific |
| spencer | woman's undershirt |
| squash | soft drink, usually orange or lemon flavored |
| stone | measurement of weight equal to 14 pounds; not used since the switch to metric, however |
| surgery | doctor's office |

| | |
|---|---|
| swat | to study hard or cram for an exam |
| tea | usually more than just a cup of tea, possibly supper |
| telly | television set |
| trifle | a dessert |
| trunk call | long-distance telephone call |
| vacuum flask | Thermos bottle |
| varsity | university |
| wag | to skip school |

## COCKNEY SLANG

Here is just a sampling of the mysterious, almost secret lingo of Londoners traditionally born within the sound of the bells of St. Mary-le-Bow church. These people were called Cockneys, and it is believed their slang was invented to outwit non-Londoners and perhaps even the police.

When using the Cockney slang, often only the first word of the two-word phrase is used, therefore assuming that the listener knows the full phrase. Example: *Bacon and eggs* refers to someone's legs. Therefore, in Cockney, someone might say, "She's got smashin' bacons."

| *Cockney* | *English* |
|---|---|
| apples and pears | stairs |
| Aristotle | bottle |
| bacon and eggs | legs |
| bees and honey | money |
| biscuits and cheese | knees |
| bottle and glass | ass |
| bucket and pail | jail |
| Cain and Abel | table |
| carving knife | wife |
| dickory dock | clock |
| dog and bone | phone |
| elephant's trunk | drunk |

| | |
|---|---|
| fine and dandy | brandy |
| German bands | hands |
| grasshopper | copper |
| hearts of oak | broke |
| iron tank | bank |
| Jim Skinner | dinner |
| kidney punch | lunch |
| Lilian Gish | fish |
| Oliver Twist | fist |
| pig's ear | beer |

These samples have been extracted, with permission, from a wonderful little booklet entitled *Rhyming Cockney Slang*, edited by Jack Jones and published by Abson Books, Bristol, England, 1991. Abson has published similar booklets, for example:

*Yiddish English/English Yiddish*

*Scottish English/English Scottish*

*Irish English/English Irish*

*Australian English/English Australian*

*Yorkshire English/English Yorkshire*

For more information, write: Abson Books, Abson, Wick, Bristol BS15 5TT, England.

## OXYMORONS

Oxymorons fall into several categories: ironies, unwitting contradiction in terms, jarring juxtapositions, pairs of incongruous words, redundancies . . . and just plain fun.

Here, in no special order, is a list collected over the past decade.

| | |
|---|---|
| closet exhibitionist | minor catastrophe |
| pseudo authenticity | probably definite |
| mournful optimist | progressive flat-tax |
| restricted free agent | perfect man |

| | |
|---|---|
| safe sex | same difference |
| pretty ugly | awfully good |
| casually elegant | passive aggressive |
| new tradition | definitely enigmatic |
| lucky S.O.B. | passive exercise |
| mandatory option | future history |
| educational television | athletic scholarship |
| congressional ethics | original print |
| cruel kindness | open secret |
| wise fool | genuine phony |
| deliberate speed | point in time |
| fair tax | white chocolate |
| Play: "Alone Together" | Book: *Intimate Strangers* |
| strategic accounting | net negative income |
| sharing secrets | prerecorded |
| learned counsel | honorable court |
| dry beer | death benefit |
| civil war | holy war |
| baby grand | freezer burn |
| mobile home | lead balloon |
| cruel kindness | hot ice |
| family vacation | moral majority |
| creative writing | working mother |
| dysfunctional family | bittersweet |
| sugar-free candy | |

And, finally, a *double* oxymoron. I once saw this sign above a bingo parlor in London:

Members Only

Free Membership

# Index